No Unseen Hands

THE STORY OF REVIVAL IN ETHIOPIA

NONA FREEMAN

UNSEEN HANDS

Unseen Hands

by Nona Freeman

©1987 Word Aflame Press
Hazelwood, MO 63042-2299
Reprint History: 1988, 1990, 1992, 1993, 1994, 1995, 1996

Art by Jo Elen Macon

Cover Design by Tim Agnew

All Scripture quotations in this book are from the King James Version of the Bible unless otherwise identified.

All rights reserved. No portion of this publication may be reproduced, stored in an electronic system, or transmitted in any form or by any means, electronic, mechanical, photocopy, recording, or otherwise, without the prior permission of Word Aflame Press. Brief quotations may be used in literary reviews.

Printed in United States of America.

Printed by

Library of Congress Cataloging-in-Publication Data

Freeman, Nona, 1916—
   Unseen hands : the story of revival in Ethiopia / by Nona Freeman.
      p.   cm.
   ISBN 0-932581-22-6
   1. Teklemariam Gezahagne. 2. Missionaries—Ethiopia—Biography.
I. Title.
BV3562.T44F74 1987
289.9'4'0924—dc19
[B]   87-23263
                                                                                      CIP

To the Author and Finisher of all completeness, the One who arranges and details and maintains the end from the beginning—Jesus, my friend—who did it all. I humbly dedicate my unworthy efforts for His glory alone.

Artist's rendering of Tekle's vision described on page 20.

Contents

    Foreword 9
    Preface 13
1. Time and Again 15
2. The Search 21
3. Called! 29
4. Moving On 41
5. God's Choice 53
6. It Came to Pass 69
7. Baptism in the Name 79
8. Beacons 89
9. The Lord Said Go 97
10. Rejection 107
11. Such as Should Be Saved 111
12. Opposition from Within and Without 123
13. In the Furnace 139
14. Molding a Church 153
15. God Sends Revival 163
16. The Lord Working with Them 177
17. Advancing in the Name of Jesus 189
18. The End Is Not Yet 199
    Appendix: The Road to Ethiopia
        by Michael Trapasso 215

Foreword

Not since the day when Philip the Evangelist attached himself to the chariot of the Ethiopian eunuch has there been so much spiritual excitement over Ethiopia. The Holy Spirit has moved mightily in the last decade. Literally thousands have come to the Spirit-filled experience. Not the least of those who have been in the forefront of the battle are our beloved Brother Tekle and his wife Sister Erkenesh. This couple has been greatly used in the miraculous, sovereign move of God in Ethiopia.

Their humble spirit is noteworthy. Constantly they are mindful to give praise to Him who called them out of darkness into this marvelous light. No doubt, the very fact that their ministry is Christ exalting is the key to the spiritual success they have had. You will not be able to put this book down. It is different!

May I add that this is Nona Freeman at her best. No one is any more knowledgeable of the Ethiopian revival than the Freemans. No one is more capable of recording it for history than our beloved Nona. She has done it again! Do not let me hold you any longer; leap right into the miraculous ministry of the twentieth century—Ethiopian style!

T. F. Tenney

There are stories that can be told, and then there are stories that must be told. This is a story that must be told.

Tekle and Erkenesh are anointed by God, directed by the Spirit, and they effectively proclaim the gospel of Jesus Christ. Their story, like their lives, is miraculous. The miracles recorded herein at times seem impossible to believe, but that is why they are truly miracles. The word *miracle* denotes a need or circumstance beyond the scope of human help. Excitement and joy come after the miracle. Were the story of Tekle and Erkenesh to be depicted on a graph, it would peak at the extreme highs of joy and dip to the extreme lows of need. The stabilizer is their perfect trust in God and their commitment to praising Him.

My life is blessed by knowing these people. I have watched them minister, visited their field of labor, been in their home, sat at their table, and shared true fellowship with them. The pages of this book invite you to do the same.

Nothing could be more appropriate than for this story to be told through the spirit and ability of Nona Freeman, a legend in her own right of faith, miracles, and praise.

Thetus Tenney

My association with the Ethiopian church began in 1971 and has been a great spiritual inspiration in my life. The Ethiopians' unreserved love and dedication to our Lord ranks them as great leaders in the faith.

Without reservation, I can say that Reverend Teklemariam Gezahagne is the greatest soulwinner I have ever known. Although I was his missionary superintendent for ten years, I always stood in awe when I witnessed his complete surrender to the Lord. We labored together in harmony and with a deep friendship.

Sister Erkenesh, Reverend Teklemariam's wife, has that quiet, sweet spirit that is so precious in the sight of the Lord. Her good cooking and kind hospitality will always be remembered and appreciated by my wife and me.

I am grateful that Sister Freeman has taken the time and effort to record these wonderful and true events. We served under the Freemans for eleven years of our foreign missions labor, and their leadership was excellent. Their close walk with the Lord has had a lasting impact for good on our lives as well as on the lives of countless others who know them. You will enjoy this book as well as her other writings.

John Harris

Preface

Ethiopia is an ancient land of grandeur and pathos. Its history is no less awesome, fearful and magnificent than its varied topography of rugged peaks, rivers, lakes, deserts, and highlands.

This true story does not chart the course of kings and emperors, or the blood and tears of political changes, or even the tragedies of famine and drought. Many events and upheavals are omitted to focus on the marvel of an "unseen hand" that has protected, guided and used two sincere, unpretentious people. Tekle and Erkenesh lead one of the most outstanding revivals of this century. Without considering adverse conditions, often ignoring facts, they move with humility and with one theme of faith:

"Ethiopia shall soon stretch out her hands unto God" (Psalm 68:31).

In lands of great antiquity a world of malevolent spirits is recognized fearfully and is given slavish submission and careful reverence. Weird and strange circumstances frequently occur that the Western mind finds hard to understand and almost impossible to believe.

This book contains several inexplicable accounts ascertained by more than one witness. I trust the reader can accept this fact: in spite of our enlightenment, there are still enormous mysteries in other regions of the world, and our limited range of experience does not encourage comprehension.

It is enough to declare emphatically that we acclaim

the One who can handle any situation regardless of its origin or extent. Jesus said, "All power is given unto me in heaven and in earth" (Matthew 28:18).

I wish to express thanks to a host of helpers, without whom this book would not have happened:

Tekle and Erkenesh, who shared their story,

Meseret, a blind brother in their church who typed it,

Nell Perry, who did editing and word processing,

Charlie Perry, who spread courage around,

Cecil Perry, who responded when needed,

Jo, who painted and shared spiritual insights,

My Bug, ever a patient bulwark of strength, and

the friends who contributed a cheerful word

of wisdom or a thoughtful deed

My heart overflows with love and gratitude to all of you.

1

Time and Again

"**S**wimmer! Call a swimmer! A boy is drowning in the river!" The woman ran toward the village yelling at the top of her voice. Then hurrying back to the river with the man who responded to her call for help, she explained what had happened.

"While I was doing my wash, I saw Tekle herding his father's cattle near the flooded river bank. Suddenly, a strange man grabbed him and flung him into the rolling waters and ran away. Oh, sir, can you save him?"

"I'll try," he answered as he tossed his clothes on the sand and plunged into the water.

Word of the happening swept the village, and an anxious crowd gathered on the bank. Just when they gave up hope and thought the raging river had claimed both lives, the swimmer crawled out with the ten-year-old slung over his shoulder and dropped him at their feet.

"Sorry," he panted, spewing water. "Too late—took so long to find him." He sprawled exhausted on the sand. Neighbors and family formed a silent circle around the lad's lifeless body. As they stood numbed by shock, a choking gasp brought hope.

"He's alive!" they shouted in glad surprise, and lifting his arms they pounded him on the back. "Look! He lives!"

Two years later Tekle climbed a sycamore tree to pick nuts. He saw the best ones in thick array at the very top of the tree. He climbed higher and higher. Suddenly, the branch he stood on snapped, plummeting him to the rocky ground far below. He lay unconscious for half an hour before he revived with a painful souvenir of his fall—a broken nose.

The same year, village leaders sent him to the summit of a nearby hill to crack a whip loudly, which (according to their custom) signaled the beginning of a festive occasion. As he snapped the whip with all of his might, it curled around a tree stump, causing him to lose his balance and fall on the stump. A dead branch of two fingers width pierced his stomach. Villagers heard his screams and carried him down the incline to his parents' hut.

Without a doctor or clinic available, they helplessly listened to his groans as he lay on a grass mat. When his father finally decided to pull the six-inch-long stick from his abdomen, he found that fatty tissue had prevented intestinal rupture. The wound slowly healed.

Not long after, in 1951, a devastating epidemic of typhoid swept the district. Tekle's mother nursed him through four months of acute illness. When he had partially recovered, she, along with several members of the family, was stricken with the disease. Now Tekle took his turn caring for those too ill to fend for themselves.

One day when he went for firewood to cook oatmeal, a hyena attacked him. He beat it off, but the slant-backed creature furiously charged him again. This time a flood of weakness engulfed him, and he could only huddle trembling on the grass. The hyena circled him, sniffing several times, before it trotted away.

The total absence of medical help cost the lives of ninety percent of the villagers. The remaining ill and dying could not bury their dead. Tekle decided that if he could move his ailing family to a higher elevation on the mountainside, away from the putrid air, they might survive.

The fourteen-year-old fashioned a crude hut of leafy branches, and with considerable effort he half carried, half dragged his patients to this shelter. By the time the repulsive hyenas found them, some of the men had recovered enough to cut poles for a more substantial abode. Though weakness prevented the men from plastering the gaps with mud as they usually did, the hyenas could do nothing more than stick their repugnant snouts through the cracks and sniff. Only one child died after they moved to the mountain.

Because of contaminated water and no crops in their village, the family moved to another district. The joy of the first harvest on their new farm turned to consternation when Tekle screamed. As he sat on a rock and held a small child, an extremely poisonous snake crawled behind him and bit him on the hip. His uncle hurried to his aid and with a sharp blade cut out the affected flesh. Gushing blood carried the venom out of his system.

While recovering, Tekle and a friend played with a machine gun that he had found in his uncle's house. They thought the bullets had been used and tossed them into the fire. They barely escaped the violent explosions that followed.

The days went by, and as Tekle herded cattle or worked in the fields, he became acutely aware of the world around him. He gazed at the awesome convolutions of craggy mountain peaks and wept; he marvelled at the symmetrical elegance of a tree. A gazelle's graceful leap or the soaring of a bird brought tears to his eyes. A growing desire to know the God who made this breathtaking beauty filled his heart.

One day he leaned backward in order to see the wide, blue-white expanse of the heavens. "O God, Creator of all these wonders," he cried, "I entreat You for only three things: first, make a way for me to learn to read and write; second, give me wealth of the world so that I can feed the poor and hungry; third, make me a priest and let me serve You all the days of my life. O God, I understand Your power by the work of Your hands. Please do not let me die before I receive these three requests."

His parents observed their disconsolate son often weeping and praying, and they were perplexed. After several months they asked, "Son, what is troubling you?"

"I want to go to the church school so I can learn to read."

They allowed him to go for a month, then came for him. "You must return home," his father said. "I need your help with the farm work."

A year later, a desperate Tekle left without permission for a nearby town, where a storekeeper hired him for a scanty wage. He regained his parents' favor by sending them the small monthly salary he earned for two years. All went well until with the aid of a mentor he enrolled in school. Angrily, his parents brought him home again to assist in the unending toil of the farm.

He helped for another year, then made his decision: "I must have an education at any cost."

Seeing his determination, his parents did not stand against him, but neither could they offer him support. His brother-in-law who lived near the mission would welcome him only as a full-time farmhand. He could not find a part-time job to provide the barest necessities. Eggs finally solved his problem; scouring the villages and farms, he bought eggs cheaply and sold them to the merchants in town for a small profit. The proceeds bought clothes and school needs, and he completed eight grades in four years at the mission school.

From age eighteen Tekle suffered a chronic type of hemorrhaging dysentery. Neither ancient apothecaries nor so-called "holy waters" nor modern doctors gave him relief. His left leg shriveled from a large boil that had him continually groaning with pain for three months. As the woman who touched the hem of the Savior's garment, he suffered many things at the hands of many physicians, even blood poisoning from unsterilized, hypodermic needles.

One day he dragged his frail body onto a rocky ledge to bask in the sunshine, utterly miserable with pain and nausea. A young boy, full of the Holy Ghost, saw him there and said in compassion, "Jesus heals, even today."

Tekle's family religion made much of the trinity doctrine, often referring to "God the Son." His full given name, Teklemariam, means "the son of Mary," but he knew nothing of Jesus. "Where in the world can I find Jesus?" he asked, bewildered.

Unseen Hands

Instantly, with open eyes he saw a vision of shimmering radiance. Just as a stone cast into water makes shining circles that expand the sea into infinite waves, so the earth increased before him to endless yellow, brown and green immensity, and the heavens above him enlarged and multiplied into luminous bands of a rose-gold glow interspersed with rounded layers of soft light. He heard a voice say, "I am bigger than this vision. I am God, and I am everywhere."

Tekle trembled as the vision faded. Turning to his new friend, he entreated, "Teach me to pray."

Instead, the lad fell on his knees, calling on Jesus to heal by His power. Tekle followed his example, praying for the first time in the name of Jesus. Soon, he felt as though two hands entered his stomach. They seemed to pull him apart. He stopped praying and cried out in anguish, "Someone is killing me—I am dying." Terror turned to despair. "Let Him kill me. After all, I am nothing more than a dead dog."

Slowly, the pain drained away. Relief came softly. It took a few moments for him to realize what had happened. He noticed the boil had disappeared, and he jumped to his feet. "I am healed!" he shouted. "The misery is gone. I am whole!"

With tears of joy the young boy and Tekle hugged each other and glorified the name of Jesus over and over.

2

The Search

Tekle was a staunch member of the Coptic church until he finished the eighth grade at the age of twenty-two. He strictly obeyed the rules of its liturgical books and loved to read them aloud daily. His healing brought a new spiritual hunger, and questions stirred in his mind.

He went to the abbot of Tekle-Haimont Monastery, located at Adua Adiabun in Tigre Province. "Which of all these books is inspired and given by God for our salvation?" he questioned.

"The Bible is the only divinely inspired book," the priest replied. "The others are the imaginative writings of men."

Stunned by this answer, Tekle exclaimed, "Then why doesn't the church condemn the liturgical books and openly declare the Bible to be the inspired Word of God?"

"The people have believed in these books by unlearned and gain-seeking men since childhood," the abbot replied. "It's impossible to turn them to the true way now. If we tell them that Jesus is the only savior of men, they would denounce us to the emperor, and he would punish us. We would be deposed from our positions and probably stoned to death. Fearing disgrace, the bishops refrain from telling the truth."

Tekle turned away, deeply disturbed. If the priests will not tell the people the right thing, he thought, I will be the first one to proclaim truth. He did not pause to consider the consequences of his action. From a rocky height overlooking the courtyard he began to weep, shout and wail loudly until he had the attention of thousands of worshipers gathered for a religious festival.

"The books taught by the clergy are false!" he cried. "They will lead you to hell, not to the kingdom of God. The priests are afraid to tell you the truth; their god is their bellies!" He continued, "The Bible alone is the Word of God! I am ready to die after I tell you the truth. Cursed be all other books but the Bible! Cursed be everyone who does not love Jesus!"

Priests and people converged on him in fury and began beating him with sticks and iron rods, trying to kill him. Suddenly, one of the priests threw himself over Tekle, crying to the people, "I command you by the name of the saints, Tekle-Haimont and Abbo not to shed this cursed man's blood upon this holy ground."

The crowd fell back. The priests delivered him to his parents, who took him home, beat him severely, disowned him and forbade him ever to set foot in their village again.

Driven away from family and friends, Tekle found himself alone and desolate. The unseen hand that had protected him this far moved on a stranger in Adua to give him six *birr* every month for the next two years. (The Ethiopian monetary unit is the *birr,* which is currently

The Search

about half the value of the U.S. dollar.)

Tekle took the national examination for entrance to the government high school, but he feared his score would be less than the required 70%. When a newspaper showed his name with a grade of 87.2% on a list of accepted students, he jumped up and down on the street and praised God with a loud voice. He did not care what anyone thought or said. No more eggs! The government would give him a grant that would provide food, lodging and an allowance for other needs.

Tekle's spiritual quest began in earnest after high school. He studied at the Lutheran Bible College for four years, completed correspondence courses offered by the Seventh Day Adventists and took two summer programs at the Mennonite Bible Academy in Nazareth. He rejected an offer for a degree program in a Lutheran school of theology because he was troubled by the human philosophies the Lutherans taught and by their way of discrediting biblical miracles.

He asked the dean of a Bible college, "Which one of all the Christian churches is the true body of Christ that will go in the Rapture?"

"Maybe in the end God will unite the good ones from all Christian churches and make them one church in the air," answered the dean.

Disappointed and grieved by the answer, Tekle returned to his room and wept in prayer, "O Lord Jesus, please do not be angry with me. Out of the many churches who supposedly worship You, I beg You to reveal Your true church to me. And, dear Lord, until You give me the right answer and lead me to the true church, I will not attend any church; I will not read the Bible, nor will I pray."

In the next few days he sold some of his theological books, destroyed those he could not sell and put his unread Bible away in a box.

His answer came a month later in a strange way. He heard it only in his right ear. "Wasn't Peter saved? Wasn't Paul saved? Were not all of the apostles saved? The doctrine that saved the apostles will also save you." The words repeated continually in his ear for three weeks, and he began a diligent search for a church that taught the apostles' doctrine.

An excited young man came to Tekle in 1963, telling him that God was literally pouring out the Holy Ghost as stated in the second chapter of Acts. "Many have received the Holy Ghost in Addis, even as Peter quoted from Joel the prophet: 'And it shall come to pass in the last days saith God, I will pour out of my Spirit upon all flesh.' You may have this gift if you are hungry."

"How can the Holy Ghost enter the heart of men?" Tekle argued. "He is the third person of the Trinity who possesses a distinct personality in the form of man. Haven't you read in Genesis 18 that the Trinity appeared to Abraham, ate and drank with him and had their feet washed? How on earth can you say that one of the Trinity can be 'poured out' on men?"

"Let us forget the teachings of men," the young man insisted. "Believe with me that without a doubt the Holy Ghost is poured out on men. I have seen with my own eyes how the Spirit changes the lives of men after they receive the promise of God; I cannot doubt."

"Is this in my Bible?" Tekle demanded. "Can you show me this in my own Bible, or do you have another

Bible? If the Bible tells of the Holy Ghost being poured out, surely my Bible school teachers would have taught me about it."

"Leave those so-called teachers to their trade in the name of the Bible. I can show this wonderful thing to you in your own Bible," the young man answered. He then showed Tekle three passages of Scripture and left him.

While on his knees Tekle read the four Gospels and the Book of Acts. He underlined the verses that referred to the Holy Ghost or the Spirit. When he found forty-two references to the Spirit in Acts alone, Tekle saw the absurdity of his ritualistic faith and realized his need to be filled with the Spirit. He went to the young man who had witnessed to him. "Now tell me how you received the Holy Ghost and how I may also," he requested.

"I have not yet been filled with the Holy Ghost," the young man admitted.

"Then how can you testify about it without having the experience?"

"Because I saw my friends at the university and at Teacher's Training College filled with the Holy Ghost, speaking in other tongues and prophesying. Their wicked lives have changed completely, and now they worship God with tears and with humility."

Because of college entrance examinations, Tekle could not take the two-day bus ride to Addis to see for himself until September, 1964. After arriving, he saw numbers of young people rejoicing in the liberty of the Holy Ghost at the Finnish Pentecostal Mission. His desire to receive the Pentecostal experience increased. He took the hands of those who had been filled, pressed them down firmly on his head, and cried with a loud voice, "Holy Spirit, come upon me! Holy Spirit, come!"

He thought it would be like an electrical shock transmitted by their hands. After seven futile attempts he thought, "Oh, the hands of the laymen will not work. Let me go to a missionary. It will come through her."

He asked an elderly missionary, Mrs. Helvy, to lay her hands on his head while he pressed down as hard as he could. Nothing happened. Running from the church in anguish, he counted himself the chief of sinners and feared that God would strike him dead with a thunderbolt for daring to enter the presence of holy people.

He bought a hundred-page notebook and recorded all of the sins from Genesis to Revelation. He purposed to go naked and barefoot from church to church, to all monasteries, to mosques and city squares to confess all the sins that he had written, even those he had not committed.

Missionary Stocks saw him writing and questioned him. When Tekle told him what he planned to do, he took the book out of his hands and read it, for he understood Amharic. "Come home with me, Tekle," he said.

At his residence, Mr. Stocks took a match and burned the notebook. "The blood of our Lord Jesus Christ has burned your sins on His cross as I am burning this book," he explained.

Though very upset, Tekle did not want to add the sin of insulting a missionary to his other wrong deeds. He left Missionary Stocks' home immediately; however, when he tried to list the sins again, he found it impossible to do so.

His intense desire to have the Holy Ghost compelled him to think of something else that might help. I'll go to

The Search

the village of Debre-Zeit, fifty kilometers away, he thought. I'll go into the woods and lie on the dew-wet grass all night and pray. Surely then, God will have mercy and pour His Spirit on me.

Just as he situated himself face down on the grass in the night illumined by a pale moon, he heard a house owner load his gun. (The man had seen Tekle slipping into the woods and thought that he must be a thief.) At that very moment the glint of a moonbeam revealed an enormous python slithering through the grass toward him. If the python swallows me, there'll be nothing for my relatives to bury, he thought, but if the man shoots me, they can claim my dead body.

Having chosen his course of action, he jumped up and ran. Trying to get away, he fell into a huge pit that had been dug for a latrine. He had eluded his pursuer, but he now faced the difficult task of getting out of the straight-sided hole. After several futile efforts—bruised, but without broken bones—he managed to scale the walls. Covered with mud and stinking filth, he found a hill of refuge and water to wash himself and his soiled clothing. In the early morning he waited under the trees until his clothing "drip-dried."

Tekle returned to Addis by bus on September 10, 1964. He had fasted three days by this time. While standing near the university gate in the afternoon, he heard a commanding voice say, "Run!" He hesitated, looked around, but saw no one. "Run!" the imperative voice came the second time. "Run to the Finnish Pentecostal Church."

A strong desire to run overwhelmed him. As he ran he thought, If I meet an acquaintance and he asks, "Why

Unseen Hands

are you running? Why are you weeping?" I will not know how to answer. Perhaps I should stop running and walk. His feet refused to cooperate with his mental decision, however. More than five kilometers from where the word came to run, he entered the church with a desire to kneel. He thought he must have knelt on an electric wire; before his second knee touched the floor, the Holy Ghost fell on him as a mighty waterfall of glory. In an ecstasy of joy he felt the power of God lift him into heavenly places. With uplifted arms he spoke in other tongues for five hours.

When the irrepressible flow of the Spirit abated, he still could speak only in tongues. He spent the next twenty-four hours trying to communicate by sign language. His relatives considered taking him to a mental hospital; he could not make them understand that he felt weak and desperately hungry. When his mother tongue—Tigrinya—returned, he talked constantly, hoping this would assure him of not losing the ability to speak it again.

3

Called!

Boundless joy came to Tekle with the baptism of the Holy Spirit. He spent his days in prayer, praise and witnessing. He felt the love of God burning intensely in his heart, and often he prayed through the night. On October 11, a month after his Spirit baptism, he had a vision of a hand extended from heaven holding out a Bible to him. The voice he heard came so definitely and vividly that he would remember the exact words from that time on.

"I have chosen you to preach My word to Ethiopia. Do not become a salaried preacher as long as you live. Do not let missionaries snare you with money; and until I reveal the right church to you, do not affiliate with any religious organization. If you hold fast to My promise in Matthew 6:24-34, I will bless you richly on earth, as I did Abraham, and give you everlasting life when this life is over."

The call bewildered Tekle. He considered himself too young and lowly for God's service. Who would listen to

Unseen Hands

him if he tried to preach? Surely Satan has sent this manifestation to delude me, he reasoned. For two weeks the vision hovered before him continually, creating such turmoil in his mind that he could not go anywhere or even converse with his friends.

He rebuked the vision often, but it did not fade until he consulted with a missionary. "Brother Cubarn, I have a problem. I cannot tell you what it is, but please pray to the Lord about it and tell me what He reveals to you."

"Why don't you tell me, Tekle?"

"No, I will not discuss it," he answered stubbornly. "Let the Lord show you."

When Mr. Cubarn saw him coming the next morning, he ran rejoicing to meet him and gave him a hearty hug.

"Listen to what the Lord has said: 'I am Alpha and Omega, unchanging Jesus, Lord and God. I have called my servant to minister the gospel. He will bring the shining light of truth to this people. Tell him not to doubt, but to go to Mekele and dedicate himself to the ministry. I will be his shield and lead him in the way I want him to go and will provide for his needs.' He also told me to give you twenty birr for your transport to Mekele."

I have always believed Mr. Cubarn to be a sincere man of prayer, Tekle thought. How could he be deceived if he has the same message I received? Still resisting the call, however, he responded, "Why wouldn't God rather call respected men for His service—men such as bishops and monks?"

"No, Brother Tekle, God calls whomever He wills," the missionary answered sternly. "I have heard from the Lord. God, not Satan, told you this thing. You must obey

Called!

the voice of the Lord without doubting. If you are disobedient, you may even die. I ask you to consider your decision seriously."

Shaken by the missionary's words, but still doubting, Tekle decided to ask God for a sign. He prayed in his heart (lest Satan hear) the most unlikely thing he could think of: "Lord, let someone else give me fifteen birr this very day for a bus ticket to Mekele. Then I will believe that the vision and the call came from You."

He went to the center of town and saw a friend, Gebra Haywat. As they greeted, the man took fifteen birr from his pocket and put it in Tekle's hand. Tekle stood in shock for several moments, unable even to say thank you. Why did I come this way? he wondered.

Mr. Cubarn asked him to testify in the afternoon service, and he felt God's anointing as never before. Later, searching his pockets for money to pay a bill at a restaurant, he found an envelope containing 150 birr. His thoughts whirled in agitation. This is a test to see if I will return it to the chapel. . .or maybe it's counterfeit money.

He found a note from a missionary lady tucked between the bills: "God told me to give you this money for whatever you need." Altogether, he received 195 birr that week in unexpected gifts.

Four days later Tekle saw Mr. Cubarn again. "How long will you be stiff-necked and hesitate to do God's will, Tekle?" he questioned. "Spend the night with me tonight, and I will see that you get on the bus for Mekele tomorrow."

On the bus Tekle felt moved to testify to the man sitting beside him. The man, deeply moved, began to weep and pray. When the bus reached the man's destination, the steward had to insist that he get off.

"Are you an angel or a man?" he asked Tekle, giving him a farewell hug. "Until today, my hope lay with idols and gods who cannot save. As you spoke to me, I heard Jesus say, 'I am the only God and your only savior.'"

Tekle witnessed to the passenger who took the first man's place until they reached Desse, where the bus stopped overnight. "Let us share a room," Tekle suggested, "so that I can tell you more." They prayed throughout the night.

When they reached Mekele at five o'clock the next afternoon, Tekle felt as though an enormous weight suddenly lifted from his head. He danced like a frisky calf down the street to the chapel where he had led services as a student. The group gathered for prayer welcomed him warmly, and he ministered to them.

He had pleasant memories of the city of his school days, when he had not known financial anxiety. Now he found it a place of liberty to preach in peace. The next day he made a year's contract with a lady to provide him with food, which took most of the money that he had brought with him. She served a piece of bread and a cup of tea for breakfast and a small loaf of *enjera* with a bowl of bean soup for both lunch and the evening meal. (Enjera is a pancake made from *teff,* an Ethiopian grain staple.)

The following week he found his friends Amare and Hailu on the point of quitting school because they did not have money for food. "No, no," Tekle said. "You must not leave; I will share my food."

One of them ate breakfast, the other two divided the

lunch, and all three shared the evening meal. By the end of the year, with God's blessing and in spite of the skimpy meals, none of them had lost weight or suffered from malnutrition.

Tekle preached the saving power of Jesus, the baptism of the Holy Ghost with the evidence of speaking in other tongues, divine healing and deliverance. He determined to reach every person in the city regardless of position or rank. Many found it difficult to believe that he would work so hard without support. The more suspicious ones alerted friends in the bank and in the post office to let them know if he received funds from unknown sources. The realization that he lived strictly by faith opened many hearts and doors. The last six months of his year in Mekele, Tekle saw numbers healed and filled with the Holy Ghost.

A man of Ethiopian-Italian descent worked as a mechanic in a sugar factory at Wonji. One night he saw something open his bedroom door. He cried out in terror, "Who are you?" Instantly the apparition turned into a white cat and disappeared. Several times during the night the cat returned to claw him on the arm, always vanishing as he tried to hit it. Deep, angry scratches proved that the experience was more than just a nightmare.

When seven months in the hospital failed to cure his excruciating headaches and dispel his torment, the man was committed to an insane asylum. He escaped to haunt taverns, drinking heavily. He could disappear without paying the bill as neatly as the white cat that tortured him.

The demon in him would often cause the man to run at unbelievable speeds for long distances. Eyewitnesses claim that he ran 130 kilometers behind a car from Addis Ababa to Debre-Berhan. Friends there bound him with ropes and took him to Mekele. He got away from them and lived in the forest with wild animals, making forays into town to satisfy his thirst for liquor.

One day Tekle found him on the street. Knowing that he could not pray there, he clasped the man's hands tightly and commanded the devil to take the man to his place of lodging. Later, while Tekle fasted and prayed in his room for the unfortunate man, someone told him that a crazy man sat on his doorstep and that he should chase him away. He opened the door and rejoiced to see the object of his earnest supplications to God. He led the miserable wretch to his room and laid him on his bed, ignoring the stench from his unwashed body and his long, matted hair.

The sight terrified Tewolde, Tekle's alcoholic brother, and Getachew Gebre, a Pentecostal friend, when they returned and found Tekle praying for the filthy creature.

Tekle paused to warn Tewolde, "The demon will come out of this poor man and will enter into you, unless you repent of your sins and give your heart to Jesus."

Tewolde fell on his knees and wept earnestly. Tekle interceded, wrestling in prayer for deliverance. The Lord gave a twofold victory: the alcoholic repented of his sins, and the crazy man's mind returned to normal. As he sat up and looked in wonder around the room and then at the three young men, he asked, "Where am I?"

"You are in the city of Mekele, and we are your friends in Christ," Tekle answered with tears of joy. Tekle washed the man's pathetic body and gave him a coat. Getachew contributed a pair of pants, and they took him

Called!

to the barber shop for a hair cut.

As the man's strength returned, he witnessed to the whole city of the mighty power of Jesus that delivered him from Satan and restored his understanding.

"God has sent a man to our town who can heal even the insane!" the people shouted in amazement. They brought their sick and afflicted; many found peace with God and received healing and deliverance.

At the end of the year Tekle felt that he should go to Wollo Province. On the way he preached at Maychew, Korem, Alamata and Woldiya. In a village near Woldiya he saw the people worshiping a grove that surrounded a sacred oak tree. No one could come near the tree except its priest, who regularly oiled it with butter and sprinkled it with blood. If any other person touched it, he would be killed at once. Without knowing this, Tekle broke off one of its branches. He saw the crowd running toward him and happily thought, The Lord is sending people to hear the Word. Then he saw their angry faces and the threatening axes and spears in their hands.

The power of God evidently restrained them when they came near, for they could only stare at him with intense animosity.

"Please sit down on the grass," he requested courteously, "and listen to what I have to say."

They reluctantly sat and glowered at him, still clutching their weapons.

"Would you please tell me the story of this tree?" he asked.

Everyone shouted at once, "This tree has been our great god for many generations—for our forefathers and for us."

"Does this tree have edible nuts?"

"Neither we nor our fathers before us have eaten its nuts."

"Can its branches be grafted?"

"We have not seen its branches grafted."

"Which one do you think is bigger," Tekle pointed, "this tree or the mountain yonder?"

They looked at the mountain thoughtfully and replied, "The mountain is larger."

"Now, tell me," Tekle asked, "is the mountain or the heaven bigger?"

All of them gazed at the sky and answered, "It must be the heaven."

Praying silently, Tekle phrased the most important question of all. "Is the heaven or the Creator of the heaven bigger?"

Everyone fell silent. The scowls had vanished. Finally an old man said, "The one who created the heaven must be the greatest of all."

Tekle exclaimed with a happy smile, "I worship this big Creator of the heaven and the earth, and I have come to tell you about Him."

As he talked about the almighty, invisible God, an elder interrupted him, "We have heard of an invisible God. Long ago, one of our ancestors worshiped him. His neighbor who prayed to the oak tree always heard him call on a God in heaven. Famine came. Many of those who venerated the oak tree died, but the man who called on the God of heaven had a visitor clothed in light as bright as the sun bring him a bag of money. The man and his family bought food and lived. My parents told me this story when I was a child." He turned to the crowd, "What this stranger is telling us about the invisible God is true."

With their hearts opened to him by the elder's story, Tekle arranged services in a school nearby. At the conclusion of those meetings, the oak tree did not have one worshiper left.

Moving as the Spirit led, Tekle returned to Mekele for two weeks to strengthen the believers, supported by Tewolde and Getachew. Next, he went to Adigrat, near the border of Eritrea Province. Strong Catholic influence did not hinder his faith; without a coin in his pocket he rented a large hall and advertised a revival meeting.

A hundred people came the first night, and attendance increased nightly as numbers received the Holy Ghost. Many found healing and liberation from demonic power. In the second week Tekle met persecution for the first time. The police arrested him for preaching without permission from the authorities. (This was in 1966.)

The preacher had suddenly disappeared. The new believers would have gladly brought him food, but they did not know that the police had thrown him into prison. Fleas and bugs along with the pangs of hunger and the dreadful smell of vomit and excretion from drunken prisoners tormented him for five days before a relative bailed him out. God helped him settle his accounts before he went to Senafe for a week of services.

He spent the next month in Asmara, the capital of Eritrea, preaching in different mission chapels. The Holy Ghost fell like precious rain.

"Come to Mandefera and preach in my home. You will find hungry hearts." The invitation came from Shewit and her uncle Kaleab. He first met them in the meetings at Mekele early in 1966.

Conviction of sin and a deep hunger for more of God brought numerous believers together for lengthy, earnest sessions of prayer and fiery preaching. Many received the Pentecostal experience.

"Sir, Jesus is giving the Holy Ghost to those who are hungry today, just as it happened in Acts, chapter two," Tekle testified to the Coptic bishop living next door.

The man reacted angrily, "How dare you try to teach me! You are ignorant and unlearned, and I command you to stop preaching at once."

When Tekle ignored his order, the bishop went to the authorities and accused the group of assisting rebels who had consistently tried to bring about the secession of Eritrea from the motherland. He declared that sophisticated weaponry was stored in Shewit's house and would be used to blow up the nearby army camp.

At midnight, a brigade equipped with heavy artillery came to destroy Shewit's house and its occupants, who were having an all-night prayer meeting. When Tekle and his men looked out the window and saw that death surrounded them, they called on the name of Jesus. Tekle said loudly, "I rebuke you in the name of Jesus."

The Lord touched the hands of the army and bound them, making them unable to fire a weapon. Some cried out, "My hands! I cannot move my hands! What has happened to me?"

The Lord told Tekle to preach to them.

A mighty anointing moved on Tekle as he declared the love of Jesus and His saving power. He concluded, "Now if you will all repent and pray together, I will ask Jesus to loosen your hands."

When they cried to the Lord for mercy, He released

Called!

them, and they made a hasty retreat.

Furious over the failure of his plan, the bishop arranged for teams of Coptic sympathizers to rain stones on the iron roof during every service. He gave a man 200 birr to kill Shewit on her way home from school. As she walked alone through thick woods, a man brandishing a deadly knife sprang from behind a bush. At the point of attack, something (an angel?) made him start spinning around and around. She ran toward safety but looked back several times and saw him whirling like a top. He disappeared from the community. However, persecution against Shewit and her family intensified until they felt compelled to move to Addis Ababa.

Tekle returned to Mekele in a spiritual vacuum of exhaustion and inadequacy. His desperate need to fast and pray led him to a cave where he could lay prostrate before the Lord, undisturbed for hours at a time.

On a day of weeping and groaning, a vision of hell came before him. He saw the huge, repulsive figure of Satan standing up to his waist in a violently boiling lake of fire. He reached toward the multitudes of people; with enormous hands he grasped thousands in one sweep and tossed them into the bubbling fire behind him. Tekle viewed the torments of the lost for three hours, then begged, "O Lord, please remove this sight from before my eyes."

A vision of the New Jerusalem followed. It glowed with a sparkling radiant glory. The palace in the midst of the city outshone the sun in dazzling resplendence. A long bridge spanned the distance from the world to the city of God. Throngs waited their turn at the foot of the bridge, some clad in sparkling white, others in filthy rags.

Unseen Hands

Only the white robed made it across. The bridge broke apart and the unclean fell into the lake of fire; it rejoined to allow the righteous safe passage over the chasm. The sight hovered before him for three hours.

At the end of the visions a burden for the lost engulfed him. His eyes became fountains of tears. He felt something missing in his knowledge of God. "O Jesus, I beg You to reveal Your whole truth to me."

As his time apart with the Lord ended, Tekle lamented, "If only thousands could be saved at one time. If only I had the wings of a dove and could hover over the crowds in the markets and preach to them about salvation in Jesus Christ."

One of the early crowds.

4

Moving On

"God told me to give you this," the man explained while stacking three big boxes before Tekle, who had come to the Tigre Province seeking direction. The boxes contained two large horn loudspeakers, a microphone and an amplifier.

"Praise the Lord!" Tekle exclaimed. "He did not give me wings as I asked, but something better—a voice that will reach thousands."

He went to markets, schools and public places with this gift. His audiences numbered between ten and thirty thousand. On a visit to Adwa, his home town, he found multiplied thousands of students and teachers gathered at the Queen Sheba School to celebrate United Nations Day. The principal gave Tekle permission to preach.

His sermon had hardly begun when seven demon-possessed people started gnashing their teeth, foaming at the mouth and screaming. Several shouted, "Call the town ambulance!" Others dragged the unfortunates to Tekle, who cast the demons out in the name of Jesus.

Immediately, people converged on him, calling him a healer and telling him of wretched cases of insanity in their families. "My brother is mad and bound with chains at my house," one said. "Please wait until I can bring him."

The multitude seeking miracles dismayed Tekle; he began preaching salvation stronger than ever and telling the people, "When you believe and obey the gospel, healing power in the name of Jesus will be available to you. He alone is the healer."

Though no one knew of Tekle's needs, the Lord impressed the school principal to take a large offering for him so that he could continue with his evangelistic ministry.

By 1967 over forty thousand young people across Ethiopia had received the baptism of the Holy Ghost. Efforts to organize stirred among them. The next two years saw ten thousand more added to their number. They finally agreed on a name—Full Gospel Believers—and they chose seven leaders with co-equal authority. Tekle remained a key man and a favorite preacher among them but refused to be a part of the system because of his call.

Miracles abounded. In one service a lady came who had suffered for twenty-two years with a peculiar constriction of her internal organs. She could retain only a minute amount of the liquid on which she lived. Though married for twenty years, the strange adhesions prevented her having a child. When Tekle rebuked the demons in her, they came out screaming that they were eighty thousand strong. Healed and delivered, she had a baby one year later. Several epileptics and other diseased folks found deliverance in that same service.

Moving On

Word spread of wonders done in the name of Jesus, and people streamed to the fellowship in such numbers that the state church became alarmed and launched severe persecutions against the Pentecostals. Enraged church leaders ordered many of them cruelly beaten, castrated, strangled, or thrown into prison. This effectively stopped the huge campaigns in rented buildings and scattered the believers into home churches.

Sadder than the atrocities, though, were internal weaknesses that brought division. Moved by jealousy, church leaders sent a man to one of Tekle's meetings to "prophesy" against him.

The man stood and spoke as though moved by the Spirit, "Thus says the Lord. You who sow tares among My people, I will deliver them from your hand, and I will deliver you to death and destruction. Return to your flock, my people, and beware of this deceiver."

Tekle and the congregation chose to ignore the "prophecy," and the service continued with God's blessing. Not long afterward, the so-called prophet preached at a conference in Awasa. Suddenly he fell to the floor with blood and foam gushing from his mouth. Tekle and the whole church fasted and prayed for him, but he died insane three years later.

From the time the leaders began to follow their own imaginations, the revival waned. Tekle witnessed a travesty in an all-night prayer fellowship that the Lord led him to observe but not to take part in. A demon-possessed man started shrieking early in the evening, and all except Tekle rebuked the devil in various ways. The evil spirit recognized the lack of firm faith and did not vacate the man's body. Though the man came from Haragie

Province and knew no one (he had been in the city only three days), the demon in him began calling names.

"You, sister, come and stand on my back; and I'll leave this man."

She came saying, "Blood, blood, blood!" He tossed her almost to the ceiling. She landed on the floor in immodest confusion.

One by one, he called names and gave instructions, and in every case, the one singled out was thrown about and embarrassed. He spoke to a timid young man about 3:00 a.m. and said, "If you do not leave the room at once, I will enter into you." The young man dashed out and shivered on the back porch the remainder of the night.

About daybreak, the demon in the man said, "Go to Harar [525 kilometers east of Addis] and find the rooster that has enchantment on his head. Shed his blood on this man's head, and I will come out of him." The group admitted failure and gave up trying to oust the devil.

A Lutheran family whose children had received the Holy Ghost opened their home to Tekle for meetings. One night, when the lady of the house became ill, they called Tekle to come and pray for her.

One of her daughters said, "Brother Tekle, I dreamed that my mother died and that the Lord brought her back to life and that she had a baby boy afterward."

As they knelt in prayer around the mother's bed, she died. Remembering the dream, Tekle continued to pray. After thirty minutes he felt her body become warm. He urged the others not to slack in prayer; a few moments later life returned, and she opened her eyes. She had a son a year later.

Revival exploded at Debre-Zeit. The Holy Ghost came

Moving On

as a flood on hungry hearts. In every service demons fled and miraculous healings occurred.

Seeing the throngs crowding Yehdego's large home, the bishop of the Coptic church stirred his followers to angry action. Six thousand fanatics armed with gasoline, matches, and clubs came to the house with plans to burn alive the people inside. Warned by God, the believers jumped through the windows and ran out the doors. The mob attacked the fleeing believers with clubs and fists. Some jerked up fence posts with nails in them to use as weapons.

Most of the believers left their Bibles as they fled; however, the sight of an open Bible in Tekle's hand infuriated the men beyond measure. Several beat him with fence posts until blood gushed over the Bible and he fainted. Half scalped, with a flap of skin and hair hanging by his right ear and covering his right eye, and with blood pouring from his head, he (still clutching his Bible) recovered enough to stagger away. An unknown army officer put him on a cart and pulled him to the hospital.

The bishop ordered the burning of Yehdego's household effects and the Bibles. While the flames leaped high, he yelled, "You who say 'Hallelujah' and 'Praise the name of Jesus,' I bind you by the power of the Holy Trinity on earth and in heaven. Your souls are condemned to hell!"

Tekle lay unconscious for a week while the saints fasted and prayed for him and for Yehdego, who was confined in prison. Two weeks later Tekle resumed his ministry, and the authorities released his host from jail.

One week after the attack a demon came to torment the bishop. He blabbered incessantly, "Because you dealt atrociously with the people who say 'Hallelujah,' I am come to torture you." He gnashed his teeth and screamed for a week until he died.

Tekle's blood did not fall to the ground in vain. A strong church with continuous revival shines there today.

Tekle called for a week of fasting and prayer at Tekle-Ab's house. As they sought God together, an angel appeared visible to all in a glow of brilliant light that filled the house. Some of those present fearfully tried to hide under the furniture. Tekle trembled until the heavenly messenger disappeared without speaking. Three days later, the same angel came as he prayed alone. He noted the gracious expression of his face, but the angel gave no message.

Still fasting, Tekle was praying in a closed room a week afterward when a deafening roar approached him. Fearing he would be crushed, he tried to shrink away. Then the sound changed to the gentle hum of bees buzzing, and a voice said, "Go to Awasa! Go to Awasa! Go to Awasa!"

While preparing for the journey to Awasa, Tekle prayed in the same room, and a thunder of sound like a mighty waterfall fell on him and rolled him across the room. He felt it penetrate his body with the smooth feel of oil. The powerful roar returned and covered him, entering in gentleness to the very marrow of his bones. When he heard the sound coming the third time, he stretched his arm toward heaven and cried, "It's enough, Lord. It's enough." When he realized this came for a blessing and was not designed to kill him, he regretted curbing the power of God.

That day Tekle used his last six birr for bus fare from Addis to Awasa in Sidamo Province. He did not know

Moving On

Oromo and Sidamo, the main languages of the province. He faced many cultural differences from those of his own village, 1300 kilometers away.

Nomadic cattle herders, speaking Oromo, live in the southeastern part of the province. They regard their traditional chief as god. Whenever death makes a new ruler necessary, for the next eight years they throw all of the newborn babies to the hyenas, believing that otherwise everyone will die.

A smaller Oromo-speaking ethnic group would castrate any man outside their clan who fell into their hands. Since a certain number of victims were supposed to be found before they could marry, the men prowled, on the lookout for prey continually.

A large segment of the population speaks Sidamo and eats a staple called *inset,* unknown in other places and sometimes called "false banana." They peel and grate the roots and stems of the bushes and press out the moisture. Both the fluid and the solids are placed in a hole in the ground lined with leaves of the plant. The hole is closed, and the food is left to mature for several months. It becomes cheeselike in texture and develops a repulsive odor. The people remove amounts as needed for the family meals.

Tekle's empty stomach growled as he stepped off the bus in Awasa. He saw a cross hanging on a wall and thought, This is a mission; maybe they will receive me. He found the missionary family having lunch, and they questioned him between bites as they continued eating. Finally, in desperation he asked, "Please, madam, could you give me something to kill my hunger?"

The lady became so angry her hair seemed to stand

Unseen Hands

on end. Her husband told her in Swedish to throw him a bit of food. She tossed him three small pieces of a biscuit—all three less than a mouthful. When he dared to ask for more, she stormed out the room.

Disappointed, Tekle decided to go to the villages. A twelve-kilometer walk brought him to Wando-Ghennet, where he found a friendly preacher.

"How did you dare come here alone?" his host asked. "You might have fallen into the hands of the castraters."

"I felt confident the Lord would take care of me," Tekle answered. "Would you interpret for me? I want to preach to the people gathered at the evening market."

His new friend agreed, and over four hundred people responded to the message. Tekle and his friend walked through the market.

"What is that awful smell?" Tekle asked, wrinkling his nose as his empty stomach rolled in protest.

"Oh, that is inset, our food," the man answered as he looked at Tekle closely. "But you are ill. Let us return to my home."

For four long, miserable days Tekle retched and suffered, unable to think of eating or drinking anything.

"What kind of food did you eat in the place where you grew up?" his concerned host asked.

"Peas, beans, barley and other grains," the sick man whispered, longing to taste again the food of his childhood.

With difficulty the preacher found some barley, had it ground in his presence, and put it in boiling water. Slowly, Tekle's strength returned as he sipped the barley water.

"I must pray about this matter of food," he thought. "O Lord, please give me a stomach ready to eat whatever is set before me. Make me like all kinds of food, and strengthen me with what I eat. Make me strong to serve You." Tekle felt something leave him as he prayed, and a desire entered into him for food—any food.

At once he asked his host to serve him anything they had. His wife brought him a glass of sour milk. The glass, encrusted with filth, looked as though it had never been washed. Even worse, four dead flies floated on top of the thick milk. Without hesitation he drained the glass, flies and all. Prayer made the difference. From that time on, partaking in faith, he never considered the condition of food or drink set before him.

Tekle traveled widely in Sidamo, preaching in villages and towns. In Yirga-Alem, the capital of Sidamo, the police arrested him for not having a preacher's license. They kept him at the police station, giving him a handful of raw chickpeas three times a day for food. When they released him after a week, he heard that Emperor Haile Selassie would soon visit Wando-Ghennet. On April 13, 1968, Tekle waited for the emperor at a clinic and presented his problems and hindrances in preaching.

The emperor gave orders that Tekle should be permitted to preach anywhere he liked in Sidamo. When news and written orders of the emperor's permission for him to preach reached other districts, all doors freely opened to him.

With permit in hand, he preached in hospitals, schools, army camps, police stations, churches of different faiths, markets, and public squares. Because he sent the converts to join the church of their choice, all of the churches in the area showed great progress during his stay. He had no desire to form his own organization and eat of its fruit.

Before he received the apostolic truth of baptism in Jesus' name, Tekle baptized over ten thousand people with the formula "in the name of the Father and of the Son and of the Holy Ghost."

The nonsectarian approach of his ministry appealed to the different churches, and he moved freely among them in crusades. The dedication, prayer, and fasting behind every service resulted in amazing healings, the eviction of evil spirits and mighty fillings with the Holy Ghost. The state church that formerly fought him did an about face and gave him liberty to preach wherever he chose.

While Tekle fasted and prayed in a Norwegian Lutheran mission guest house in Awasa, the Spirit impressed him to write.

He asked Hailu Wolde-Tsadik, then president of the Lutheran Southern Synod, to give him a stack of paper and several pens. (This man is now presbyter of the Apostolic church in Sidamo.)

Beginning June 28, 1969, Tekle wrote for three days, without interruption, as the Holy Spirit anointed him, producing a book called *Melekotawi Hayle (Divine Power)*. He wrote about false religion versus the apostolic doctrine, wrote against heresy and worldliness, and interpreted the prophecies of Ezekiel 37-38 with respect to Ethiopia. The book was printed by a miracle, and letters from numerous people testified of blessings from its messages.

Going from place to place, preaching as the Spirit directed, eating whatever kindness provided, and sleeping wherever he found a place, Tekle lived by faith. Sometimes, he fared better under a tree or in a cave than

Moving On

in the primitive homes of rural folks.

When word came in 1969 that his mother and sisters planned to visit him in Awasa, he rented a house, believing that the Lord would supply his needs. His mother, a staunch Coptic church member, heard that the Protestants ate dog and cat meat; therefore, she refused to eat the meal served to her by Tekle's kind neighbors on the day that she arrived. She heard a dog howling in the night and thought, Oh, they are slaughtering another dog.

She felt deeply troubled over her son's departure from her faith and frequently sent elders to convince him of the folly of his ways. But she soon recognized the cat-and-dog story as malicious slander, and her attitude softened toward his change of faith.

"Will you bring that book of yours and read it to me?" she requested four days after her arrival.

As Tekle read the Bible and explained it to his mother and his sisters, the Holy Spirit moved on their hearts, and they sought God in repentance. Today, they are born-again, enthusiastic members of the church he leads. Besides deliverance from the bondage of sin, his mother received healing for a chronic stomach condition that had caused continuous vomiting for three years.

While his mother felt happy about her repentance and healing, concern over daily needs to sustain life mounted almost to panic. "Son, you do not have money for kerosene for the lamp. There's no wood for the fire, no water, and no food. How can you go on like this? Isn't it a sin to fold your hands and only pray for our daily bread?" She continued bitterly, "You are even starving us to death. We are far from our home, and we have no means of returning. Please, get a job and make a living

Unseen Hands

for us."

Just as her tirade concluded, Tekle answered a knock at the door. "God told me to give you this for the needs of your household," the man standing there said as he handed him forty-five birr. That would pay the rent and provide essentials for the remainder of the month.

"Now do you see how Jesus takes care of us, Mother?" Tekle explained, "It's not that I do not want to work, but God told me to dedicate my time to Him, and in return He promised to supply my needs."

His mother marveled at God's unique and timely provision and began to understand her son's calling.

Two months later his family decided to return to Tigre to see about their property. Tekle felt they might be too young in the faith to stand alone, so he read to them Mark 10:29-30: "And Jesus answered and said, Verily I say unto you, There is no man that hath left house, or brethren, or sisters, or father, or mother, or children, or lands, for my sake, and the gospel's, but he shall receive an hundredfold now in this time, houses, and brethren, and sisters, and mothers, and children, and lands, with persecutions; and in the world to come eternal life."

The Scripture touched them; they never returned to Tigre.

5

God's Choice

According to their custom, Tekle's parents chose a bride for him before he received the Holy Ghost. Realizing the importance of divine direction he prayed earnestly, "Lord, if this is not Your will for me, please break it up." Shortly afterward an army officer abducted and married the girl.

His parents then found an exceptionally pretty young lady to be his wife. Again, he sought the Lord for His will. A year later a court judge, newly transferred to the district, became enamored of her beauty and married her forcibly.

When he first began preaching, an English missionary lady proposed to him. He could not find the courage to say no. He tried to think positively—she could help him in his ministry. However, two unhappy years later he had to say, "Sister, I have not had peace since our engagement. I do not want to hurt you, but this is not God's will."

"I cannot hold you if you do not feel peace," she replied tearfully. "I release you."

Unseen Hands

A large group of young people met for prayer while Tekle evangelized in Asmara. One of them prophesied to him, "My son, I have given Sister _____ to be your wife." Because he felt the presence of the Lord in the prayer, Tekle took this seriously and started dating the girl, only to learn that her interests lay in worldly activities, not in evangelism.

He decided then to give up the idea of marriage and to live a celibate life. He had sought God with all of his heart and had received only changed plans for an answer; however, while praying in Addis a few weeks later, the Lord told him plainly: "I have prepared a wife for you from the southern part of Ethiopia and not of your tribe. Do not expect people to find her for you. I Myself will unite you with My choice, and you will work for Me together."

* * * * * * *

A farmer named Segaro lived in a village called Benara in Kambata District of Shoa Province. Knowing nothing of God and His Word, he worshiped demons under the leadership of his uncle, a powerful witch doctor. He grew so discontented with his bondage that he planned to kill his uncle and run away, perhaps to start a new life in another village.

The witch doctor discerned his intentions and threatened, "I will kill your sons if you do not serve me with all of your heart."

Something in Segaro rebelled against the age-old traditions of evil, even though he knew nothing else to believe in. He could not hide the deep distress of his soul; consequently, his uncle killed his two oldest sons.

He refused to yield to merciless darkness, and two more sons died. In quick succession a series of calamities came to his house—even a plague of poisonous snakes. In desperation Segaro looked up to heaven and prayed, "O God, Creator of heaven and earth, where are You? Can You not deliver me from the power of evil?"

That week he heard for the first time of a book that teaches men about the Creator. He made a two-day journey and found the Book and someone to explain it to him. Though he could not read, he brought a copy of the Book home with him.

Obtaining that Bible cost Segaro dearly. With hands tied behind their backs, those found with the Scriptures in their possession were cruelly herded to prison by the police, who frequently beat them on the tortuous two-day walk. The police confiscated Segaro's money, food, and cattle, leaving him penniless. But nothing dimmed his joy in God's Word or shook him from his determination to follow the Lord.

Chagrined by continually begging someone to read for him, he went to school at forty years of age and learned to read and write.

A great change came into his life from the time he found God's Word. He found courage to make a complete break with the servitude of wickedness. His new faith founded on the Bible made him believe that his four remaining children, two sons and two daughters, would grow up protected by God's power. From that time he lived only to pray and to testify of Jesus, His supremacy over Satan, and the liberating authority of the Bible.

During this tranquil time, Segaro joyfully welcomed a new daughter on April 23, 1947. He called her Chako,

Unseen Hands

meaning "light" in his Kambata language. Later, he changed her name to Erkenesh, meaning "reconciliation," for he said, "I am now reconciled to my God."

Erkenesh received much loving attention from her father, who freely admitted, "She is my favorite child, begotten in the only time of peace that I have ever known."

By the time Erkenesh turned three, Protestant believers had increased in Benara and had built a church where Segaro happily took his family. The church started a literacy program, and at six years of age, Erkenesh could read easy passages from the Bible.

One Saturday night, the story of Abraham offering his son Isaac as a sacrifice gripped Segaro as he read. Long after he closed the Bible and his family slept, his thoughts revolved around the father who agreed to give God his only son. Abraham did not know that God would give Isaac back; he risked losing him forever, he mused. Sacrifice is a sad word, he thought.

That Sunday morning the elder spoke on Abraham offering up Isaac. "He gave the Lord the treasure dearest to his heart," he said in closing, "and we are sending this young couple as missionaries to a distant region. Will one of you willingly offer your daughter to serve these workers for the sake of the gospel?"

Segaro had trouble breathing. His heartbeat sounded deafening in his ears. He thought surely everyone could hear it. He stood slowly, as one suddenly grown old and feeble. His voice broke and sounded strange when he tried to speak, but he finally got the words out. "I have a daughter that I love most dearly. I vow to God that I am offering her to serve the missionaries and to belong to

God's service all of her life."

His wife burst into sobs. She and Erkenesh wept together the next few days, begging him to change his mind. Sadly, with determined patience, he explained over and over, "I have promised, and I cannot break my vow."

Though six-year-old Erkenesh had cried with her mother, she had no idea of the devastating changes her father's promise would make in her life. Her parents had kept her close. Never having played with other children, she knew little of other people in the village.

She did not know the newlywed missionary couple. Wrapped up in each other, they completely ignored her on the terrifying two-day bus trip, which was her first time to ride in a vehicle. Upon arrival at their destination and disregarding Erkenesh's exhaustion and fear, her new mistress haughtily ordered her to the kitchen to make tea. The sheltered apple-of-her-father's-eye child knew nothing of even the simplest labor and had to learn quickly or suffer painful consequences.

Shoved harshly into a cruel, impatient, adult world and assigned tasks far beyond her strength and knowledge, she silently sobbed herself to sleep in the dank kitchen every night in utter homesick misery. Hope-strangling apprehension came with the dawn of every day.

The missionaries settled in a village in Arussi Province. Customs and language differed widely from those of Erkenesh's home. She missed the fields and open vistas graced with clumps of trees here and there. Their new home, deep in the forest and without fences, allowed free course to wild animals, pythons, and jumping snakes. Lepers passed the house continually on their way to and from the S.I.M. leper hospital two kilometers away. Ter-

Unseen Hands

rified by the grotesque bodies of the lepers and by the wildness of the woods, Erkenesh often prayed to die.

With never a free moment, Erkenesh, swinging the axe with all her inadequate might, chopped wood. She carried water; she fetched grain and vegetables from the distant market; she cleaned, washed, and cooked. Her guardians constantly berated her for laziness and offered no helping hand with any task.

Relatives passing by on business stopped to see her and reported her grievous condition to her parents. Her devout father felt that he could not break his vow and bring her home, but he visited her. Grief almost overcame him to see her wretched state, and with tears he begged the missionaries to treat her kindly and to send her to school, promising to pay all expenses.

After her seventh birthday, her master sent her to the S.I.M. school not far away with the conditions that all her work must be done as before and that she could not do any school work at home. This meant that she had to complete her assignments on the way to school, missing the first period. Her teachers reproached her as irresponsible, not knowing her living conditions. In discouragement one day she drank poisonous ink, hoping to die. It did not even make her sick.

While in the fourth grade and only ten years old, Erkenesh received a letter from a health assistant asking her to marry him. Without thought she said yes, but ran from him when he tried to talk to her. She tossed away the letters he wrote; students found them and spread the story, and other young men wrote her proposals of marriage.

Apprehensive that she would be abducted according

God's Choice

to the prevalent custom, her parents could only pray and grieve, still fearing to bring her home lest they sin by breaking her father's vow. Denied the one thing she wanted most in the world, Erkenesh whimpered sadly in lonely moments, "If only I could go home."

Tamru, her oldest brother, took matters into his own hands. He took her away from her inconsiderate masters and brought her to his home in Haghere-Selam, Sidamo, where he taught in a Norwegian Lutheran mission. The misty, cold climate contrasted sharply with the sunny, warm lowlands, and Erkenesh lost weight as she suffered from a continual cold. Saddest of all, the demands on her exceeded even those of the missionaries in Arussi.

Though only eleven, Erkenesh received several more proposals. Alarmed by the ever-present threat of abduction, her brother sent her to stay with a couple he had known during his school days who lived in the capital city of Yirga-Alem.

Her situation deteriorated from bad to worse. She could not do enough work to please her guardians, who treated her cruelly and refused to give her food. Too shy to confide her troubles to anyone, Erkenesh would have starved had not her classmates and perceptive neighbors occasionally shared their meals with her.

"If only I could go home." The lament beat in her mind as a dirge, until in desperation she chopped her feet with an axe while she cut wood. She thought surely her parents would take her home if they saw her wounded. Blood streamed from the deep cuts as she struggled to the house, where she fainted and lay helplessly on the kitchen floor.

No one cared enough to ask what had happened, much

less to offer help or nourishment. Without care, her feet became infected and horribly swollen, but a week later she hobbled back to school. The couple had notified the school that she wanted to quit; however, when the teachers saw the condition of her feet, they took her to the hospital, fearing that her feet might have to be amputated. They notified her brother. He came and discovered the whole story of the cruelty that she had endured.

She recovered quickly, and Tamru paid the fees for her to enter a mission boarding school. She would have preferred going home, although life at last became easier with the opportunity to study and to enjoy regular meals. She went to a garden in the school compound every afternoon and prayed, "O Lord God, please, help me to serve You always, whether I am a student or working on a job."

A little later, she added another petition: "I entreat You to prepare for me a good husband who fears God. Deliver me from one who would be insulting or cruel or a drunkard or who would want a divorce."

Though Erkenesh prayed about serving the Lord, she had little knowledge of how it should be done. She decided nursing would be one way to work for God and applied for nurse's training school after finishing the eighth grade. When these plans failed to materialize, she entered a government high school. She qualified for an allowance with a 73% score on the national examination.

The mission authorities made an exception to their rules and allowed Erkenesh to stay at the mission because of her exemplary conduct. Fearing to live alone, she felt grateful.

Peace did not last long. A friend of her brother asked Erkenesh to marry him. When she refused, her brother withdrew his financial assistance. The director of the high school, a Coptic who was afraid of her Protestant influence, made plans to cut off her allowance. She received several more proposals for marriage at the same time.

Feeling confused and forsaken, Erkenesh turned to prayer. "O Lord, You know that I want to serve You. How can I marry a man that You have not chosen for me? Please, Lord, show me Your choice of all these men wanting me to be their wife."

Suddenly, for the first time, she received a message from God: I am Jesus. Do not accept any marriage partner until I speak to you again. Until then, wait patiently.

Erkenesh had an answer for every proposal from that time: "It is not the will of God."

Without financial resources, Erkenesh borrowed money in the beginning of the ninth grade and went home, hoping to stay. Her father sent her back to school with the assurance that he would pay the bills.

She found lodging a forty-five minute's walk from the school. One evening a captain accosted her, "I want to marry you, Erkenesh."

She made no answer; trembling she hurried down the street. Now the walk to and from school became a torment of fear. A few days later, fully armed, the man blocked her way long enough to grit, "You will tell me in my house why you hate me and despise my request." The kidnapping threat terrified her all the more since she knew no one willing to help her.

A week after the captain's threat she saw a tent pitched in front of his house and many people there dressed in mourning. One told her that someone had found the captain dead in his bed. He did not commit suicide, and murder was not suspected. While Erkenesh regretted the captain's untimely death, she could not help but thank God for deliverance.

Most of her classmates boasted of their betrothals and taunted Erkenesh for not being engaged. They called her a misfit. When their sneers became unbearable, she complained to the Lord, "Why did You bind me with Your words? Please, tell me Your plans for my future." But God did not speak to her again for five and a half years.

Erkenesh tried to enter nurse's training at the end of every year of high school. She dreamed of building a clinic to give medical assistance to the poor; however, her goal eluded her each time.

Her academic success was nothing short of a miracle. An undernourished weakling, she seldom ate breakfast, never had lunch, and had to prepare her evening meal after a wearisome day and a long walk home. Exhaustion prevented her from studying at night. She depended solely on lectures and the notes she took during classes. Yet she became one of the first two girls in Sidamo Province allowed to take college entrance examinations and the only one who passed the test. Her family rejoiced over this honor and urged her to enroll in Addis Ababa University soon.

Thinking to save money for further schooling, she chose rather to teach for a year in a Norwegian Lutheran mission in Dila, Sidamo. Instead of saving money, however, she helped her family with her salary and agreed to teach for a second year. This angered her brothers, who promised to pay her way through the university, but she did not yield.

During the second year of teaching, the insistence of

God's Choice

unsuitable suitors brought her anxiety and embarrassment again. One man threatened repeatedly, "I'm waiting for my chance. I will rape you and then make you my wife. You will not get away from me."

"No more school today because of a funeral, Erkenesh," a colleague told her one afternoon. Amazed she heard that the man who threated her had died. She learned again that God knew how to deliver her from evil men.

Though Erkenesh lived a good moral life, taught Sunday school, served as a deaconess and often as a preacher, she felt utterly dissatisfied with her Christian experience. Sometimes she questioned herself, If Christ appeared now in the clouds of glory, what would happen to me? She sadly answered her own query, Hell would be my portion, not heaven.

Feeling unworthy and using a feeble excuse, she often avoided an opportunity to speak. Discouragement made her close her Bible and cease to pray for a while. During this time she met a university student who emphatically denied the existence of God. "And many of the students agree with me," he stated.

Erkenesh had planned to start university studies the following year, and this alarmed her even more. Would she sink low enough to forget God if she went? She knelt, weeping, "I call upon You today, God of Abraham! You called him before he called on You. You separated him from his kindred and blessed him. I have prayed to You these many years, yet, You do not hearken to my plea. You have only bound me by Your message not to marry until You speak. Now, it seems my soul runs toward destruction. Lord, I need an answer today, once and for

Unseen Hands

all." With this she laid her hands on promises in the Psalms and prayed over them.

That week, during a conference at the mission, she heard Tekle preach for the third time. She enjoyed the first two messages; this time he made her angry, and she walked out. "Blasphemer! The very idea of holding out an aspirin and saying, 'If you had as much faith in Jesus as you have in this pill, you would be healed of your infirmities.' He compared the great Jesus to a little aspirin tablet!"

Angrily contemplating Tekle's sermon, her eyes fell on the numerous bottles of pills and medicine on her dressing table. Malnutrition, exposure and abuse had left Erkenesh frail and with little resistance to disease. She suffered from frequent bouts with malaria, amoebic dysentery, severe trachoma, ceaseless headaches, and chronic rheumatism, to mention some of her afflictions.

While in the twelfth grade, a violent siege of cerebral malaria had confined her helplessly in bed for three months and made the doctors fear brain damage. Though she recovered, frequent recurrence still debilitated her.

Gazing at the medicine that she considered to be essential for survival, Tekle's words quickened in her heart. She asked, "Am I a true believer? If I really had faith in Jesus, why should I suffer from all these sicknesses and have to depend on tablets for the rest of my life? If I only believed. . . ." With these words, faith mounted in her heart and her prayer continued in a different vein. "O Lord God, if You will heal me, well and good; but even if You do not care to heal me, I will die in Your hands." As she spoke, she tossed the expensive prescriptions out the window until she cleared her dressing table.

God's Choice

While Tekle continued his sermon in the conference hall, Erkenesh received complete healing in her room and felt God's presence for the first time in her life. I Peter 3:3 and I Timothy 2:9-10 touched her as she read the Bible the following morning, and she immediately removed her rings, bracelets, necklaces and earrings, putting them all in a give-away pile along with the extremely short dresses she usually wore. Never again would she put on any of those things.

Tekle brought a message on the baptism of the Holy Ghost that night. Though none of the people who responded to the invitation to pray received the Spirit, joy filled Erkenesh to learn that God pours out His Spirit on men and women today.

From the time the conference ended and Tekle left Dila to preach in other towns, Erkenesh and four friends fasted and sought diligently for the Holy Ghost. Her deep hunger for the Spirit moved her with humility to sleep on a mat on the floor rather than on her comfortable bed.

After four months, the church people sent for Tekle. When he came and laid hands on them, Erkenesh and three others received the Holy Spirit. A young teacher in the mission who was praying with them began to scream in a satanic manner. When Tekle rebuked the demon in him, he stood haughtily saying, "I am a Christian and do not have an evil spirit." He left the room in anger. Though Erkenesh did not know it, he only attended the prayer meetings because of an infatuation for her.

The griefs and disappointments of her childhood had made Erkenesh reserved and distrusting, unable to make friends. Some wrongly thought her conceited, not discerning that her real problem was a hard, unforgiving heart.

When the Holy Spirit took possession, she felt turbid darkness swept out of her heart to be replaced by a luminous glow of happiness. Joy sprang up as a sparkling fountain, and peace beyond words streamed through her soul. She praised God throughout the night in a new language.

Two students had wronged Erkenesh, and she had taken revenge by slashing their grades. At six o'clock in the morning she ran to the house where they stayed, and taking them by surprise, fell on her knees before them and begged for forgiveness.

"Jesus has filled me with the Holy Spirit," she said, "and my whole life has changed. I forgive you, and you have forgiven me. This is truly wonderful." Both of them received the Holy Ghost a few days later.

Before, Erkenesh could never spend more than five minutes in prayer. Now she prayed for hours, day and night. The shy, reserved girl disappeared, and she witnessed with overflowing love to everyone she met, regardless of race, age, or position. She received a spirit of praise that swept her joyfully through the days. God revealed the agonies of Calvary to her in a dream, and her hard heart melted in compassion for the lost.

Tekle came to visit her later, and she shared her perplexity over the way the Lord dealt with her. "Sometimes as I pray, I see many things. I see visions of Jesus, and He speaks to me. Even this morning, I saw a man die and then be brought back to life."

"No doubt God has given you discernment. Continue to seek the Lord, and He will reveal the matter to you."

"Please pray for me," Erkenesh asked, kneeling. "I want to be led by the Spirit and to have spiritual gifts."

God's Choice

A tremendous force of the Spirit struck Tekle as he bowed before the Lord. Overwhelmed, he spoke softly and in awe, "God has spoken to me. He has called you for the ministry of evangelism. You will be my wife, and we will go together...."

Before he could say more, she interrupted, "This can never be. God told me five and a half years ago that I should not get married until I received further instructions from Him."

"Do not worry about it," Tekle answered. "Just pray. If it is from God, it will surely come to pass; if not, it will not happen."

Tekle going to preach.

Preaching in the market.

6

It Came to Pass

Erkenesh put off praying until she became too miserable to wait longer. The moment she fell on her knees Jesus appeared to her in a vision, saying, "You have prayed to serve Me since your childhood, and I have called you to My work. You will be Tekle's companion and help him evangelize Ethiopia."

Unconvinced, Erkenesh tried to persuade herself against the validity of what she had seen and heard. "This must be from Satan," she said doubtfully, with a long, drawn-out sigh, "and if You did speak to me, Jesus, please change Your mind."

Another vision came of a frightening, enormous, black mountain barring the way that she needed to go. Letters settled across it to form one word; *temptation.* A voice whispered in her heart, You will be tempted by human reasoning.

Questions came on the heels of that vision: How can God speak in this way? What about my job and my plans to attend the university? How can I marry a preacher who

Unseen Hands

has no house, no money and no regular appointment? How will my parents feel about this? He is a holy man; how can I live with him?

As Tekle left for services in another town, he asked, "Has God spoken to you, Erkenesh?"

"No," she denied.

He gave her a long, intense look, and opening his Bible to Daniel 12:3, he read: "And they that be wise shall shine as the brightness of the firmament; and they that turn many to righteousness as the stars for ever and ever."

He left without another word.

Erkenesh played a key role in the Holy Ghost revival that swept the Lutheran mission, testifying of the power of Jesus and praying with people whose hearts were hungry. One day as she witnessed, she surprised herself by saying, totally unplanned, "I am going to marry Tekle and help him evangelize." After she recovered from shock and accepted God's plan for her life, she felt a greater anointing than ever before.

Revival always triggers persecution, and Erkenesh became a target. The demon-possessed teacher who had stalked from the prayer meeting in anger became her archenemy, slandering her character and furiously opposing her witness. Some of her relatives believed his report that she had lost her mind.

Erkenesh decided that she would go to Awasa and tell Tekle she would marry him, since she had already unexpectedly announced it in Dila. Her parents also should be told. At home, she related the whole story, beginning with receiving the Holy Ghost and the visions Jesus gave her. She concluded, "God has called me to the ministry of evangelism and shown me that I am to marry Tekle, a full-time evangelist from the North who has nothing but the Lord and His Word."

She waited apprehensively, hoping for their approval. Her mother finally agreed without enthusiasm, but her father's face pictured sadness as he said, "Daughter, I cannot say God did not speak to you, for I have also heard His voice. I am disturbed by this strange testimony that you have received the Holy Spirit and that you plan to give up teaching and give up going to the university in order to marry a destitute evangelist. He receives no support from any organization, nor is he affiliated with any church."

He stared long into space, then asked, "What will your life be like married to him? This is a difficult matter to decide. I can neither say yes nor no now. Let me pray about it."

Disappointed not to have her father's sanction, Erkenesh returned to Dila. Her father went to S.I.M. missionaries to learn about the baptism of the Holy Ghost. The missionaries denied flatly that speaking in other tongues happens today and that it is a sign of receiving the Holy Ghost. They assured him that every believer receives the Spirit from the moment he accepts the Lord as his personal Savior.

Encouraged by her brother Tamru's declaration that Erkenesh had lost her reason, was altogether insane, and should be put in an asylum, her father rejected her testimony as a delusion. Most of her relatives agreed and turned against her, which is a disaster in a strong family-oriented society.

Erkenesh thought that when one had been reconciled to God by His Spirit that all would be peaceful. Crushed

Unseen Hands

by the name-calling, she felt the mountain's dark shadow overwhelm her again.

"O Lord," she prayed, "You have told me to leave the security of my job and marry a preacher who has neither daily bread, clothing, nor a house. What will I eat and wear? Where will we live? I am hated and rejected by my family. If I have children, how can I take care of them?

"Why is Your hand heavy against me? Have I been created for torture? And what do I know about evangelism? God, please let me die."

The divine response came with tender patience in recurring visions and through the Word. Matthew 10:36-39 challenged her: "And a man's foes shall be they of his own household. He that loveth father or mother more than me is not worthy of me. . . .And he that taketh not his cross, and followeth after me, is not worthy of me. He that findeth his life shall lose it: and he that loseth his life for my sake shall find it."

She studied the verses, thankful for explicit promises on which to stand. Mark 10:29-30 and Matthew 6:25-34 also encouraged her. Strength to forsake all came with Psalm 45:10-11.

She felt sweet assurance from the Lord: Look at the birds of the air. I can feed you as easily as I feed them. I shall bless you as I blessed Abraham, and I will multiply your descendants.

Slowly she shook off the shadows by clinging to God's promises. "Oh, please forgive me, Lord, for doubting You," she prayed with penitent tears.

Surrender did not eliminate the problems. They intensified. Her brother agreed with the teacher who opposed her that he should kidnap Erkenesh and force her to marry him.

With six young men to help him, the teacher came barging into her house without an invitation. With sneers and mockery they began to make light of the Holy Ghost experience and declared Tekle to be a liar. As they railed against her, she, not knowing the real purpose of their coming, begged them to leave. She felt as if she were hemmed in by wild animals.

They rejected her request to leave with cursing, blasphemy and more insults. Silently, she cried to the Lord to drive them away. After some time, one accomplice stood and snarled, "What do we have to do with a crazy woman?" And they stormed out.

Trembling and deeply disturbed, Erkenesh fell on her knees under the somber shadows again. "Lord, I cannot bear all of these things. It seems that since I have been filled with the Holy Spirit my sufferings are increased to more than I can endure. Please take away Your Spirit."

She felt as if the Holy Spirit left her, and simultaneously a powerful hand threw her into horrible blackness. She felt as if she were hovering over the very midst of hell. She struggled in profound anguish until consciousness returned. Realizing the dreadfulness of her words, she wept uncontrollably, begging God to forgive and to restore her in the Holy Ghost. Just when hope had almost vanished, she felt forgiving love flow over her soul.

The mountain retreated and persecution doubled. Insulting letters from relatives hurt, but she did not stumble. Her cousin who had sent her gifts during the difficult school days came to see her, armed with a pistol, saying, "I would rather kill her myself than to see her marry that poor preacher."

In her presence he said, "I have heard that you are crazy and have come to see for myself."

"Oh no," Erkenesh replied, "I am more sane than ever, and God is leading me. He has given me His great salvation and has brought Tekle into my life so we can work together for Jesus."

"You are certainly crazy," he answered. "You do not even know where he came from. He is a wanderer and a vagabond who owns nothing. God will not tell you to marry someone who will desert you when you are with child. He would not want to commit you to a life of misery."

"It is not the way you think," Erkenesh firmly stated. "I have received the Holy Ghost, and my life has been changed. If you will seek God and receive the glorious gift of His Spirit then you will understand."

He turned away in disgust. Forgetting to use his weapon, he snarled, "What can be done with a crazy woman!"

Later, when Erkenesh saw at her door the teacher who had given her so many problems, fear pulsed in her throat. She remembered his last visit vividly. Then she saw the tears rolling down his cheeks.

"I have greatly wronged you, Erkenesh, though you have done nothing against me," he confessed. "To get my hands on the letters that Tekle wrote to you, I told the clerk at the post office that you are my relative. I destroyed his letters.

"The six young men came with me to abduct you. I'm sure you recall the night, not long ago. God put such terror in my heart that I left here shaking like a leaf in the wind. Now I know the Lord is with you. He has brought every evil attack against you to nothing. Please forgive me."

She readily forgave and began to praise the Lord as never before. Six months of wavering between doubt and faith ended in a prayer of commitment: "Jesus, I know that You are truly with me. Whatever tribulation comes my way—be it hunger, thirst, hatred, death or any other thing—I will not turn back or doubt or take my life out of Your hands."

At last she had triumphed over the shadows.

Meanwhile, family opposition to Erkenesh marrying the stranger from the North grew. Both her Kambata tribe and his Tigre tribe practiced endogamy, marriage strictly within the tribe. Tekle's Christian family had no objections. "It is God's will" satisfied them, but the brothers and uncles of Erkenesh considered any violence justified to prevent the union. Numerous attempts to kidnap and even to kill her did not faze the young couple. After much prayer and consideration, they set the wedding date for August 16, 1969.

Erkenesh's brother Tamru went to bed on the night of August 5, mulling over schemes to derail their plans, and woke up the next morning a changed man. A vision put the fear of God in him. He came twenty-five kilometers from his home in Wando-Ghennet to Awasa to make peace.

"God showed me in a vision that He ordained your marriage at the time you have chosen. He rebuked me for my evil deeds. Please forgive me for all the wrong I have done, and tell me what I can do to help you."

They forgave without hesitation, and Tekle said,

"Since you have led the opposition against us, you should go to your parents, tell them your vision, and persuade them to give their permission."

"And," Erkenesh added, "we would like to have the wedding reception at your house."

"I will gladly go to our parents, and I believe they will agree. It would be appropriate to have the feast at my house, but unfortunately, I have no money for it."

"Don't worry about the money. The Lord will provide, and we will pay for everything," the young folks answered together. With the wedding ten days away, they had twenty-nine birr between them. The word *provide* had barely been spoken when a man came and handed Tekle fifty birr, the beginning of God's provision.

Within three days, a couple gave Erkenesh her wedding dress, and a man bought Tekle a wedding suit and shoes. Gifts totaling 800 birr came to them in various ways, and in another three days everything had been bought and made ready.

With the presence and approval of both their families and a host of friends, the wedding took place in the Norwegian Lutheran mission hall, and an abundant feast at the home of Tamru followed the ceremony. The Full Gospel Believers in Addis Ababa wanted the wedding ceremony repeated in their church and sent cars to bring them the 280 kilometers.

These believers had a custom that the bridal pair should make their covenant before God, but before the conclusion of the ceremony, the question must be asked if anyone present had any objections to the union. One dissenting voice would nullify the marriage contract. Unknown to Tekle and Erkenesh, opponents waited for

It Came to Pass

this opportunity to bring reproach on them.

One kilometer from the church, they saw panting runners waving them to a halt. "Stop!" they said. "You must not go to the church. As everyone waited for you there, suddenly the police came, waving batons, yelling, and kicking over benches. They hit a few people, and the crowd fled."

"Instead," someone added, "you must go to the home of your friend Tirunesh. She has prepared a wedding supper for you."

Tekle and Erkenesh celebrated the beginning of their life together peacefully, in the midst of friends and loved ones.

It came to pass!

Tekle on wedding day.

Unseen Hands

Erkenesh and Tekle on their wedding day.

7

Baptism in the Name

Tekle and Erkenesh spent their five-day honeymoon in the home of Tirunesh and saw her again at the Full Gospel Believers' church two weeks after the wedding. "There's a new missionary couple in town named Wendell; they seem to be fine people," she told them. "They live near me, close to the French Embassy. I thought you might like to get acquainted. Here's their address; I tore it out of the American bulletin."

When Tekle called that afternoon, Bobbye Wendell answered the phone and became excited when he told her that he worked as a full-time evangelist. She pressed him to come for a visit. When he agreed, she and her husband, Kenneth, immediately came and brought him to their home. A previous appointment did not allow him to stay long. Reluctantly they let him go, urging him to come again soon and to stay longer.

Their graciousness made Tekle feel that he should call them again a few days later to say that he and Erkenesh would be leaving for Awasa the next day. Sister Wendell wept as she pleaded, "Brother Tekle, we want you to come to our home one more time before you go. Brother Wendell wants to talk to you."

Her tears and the memory of the warning vision he had in 1964 made him uneasy, and he stiffened against her plea. Brother Wendell took the phone; "Come and say goodbye, my friend, until we meet again."

Tekle could not resist the warmth of the friendly voice, and as he entered the house, a spirit of prophecy swept over Sister Wendell: "This is the man I have chosen to preach My Word to the people of Ethiopia, says the Lord of Hosts." All of them instantly fell on their knees in fervent prayer.

Tekle evaded the Wendells' request for his address in Awasa, thinking, I'm afraid to continue this friendship. They might expect me to work with them.

"Quickly, Mark," Sister Wendell hurried her son the following morning. "Take these tracts to the house where Tekle is staying."

It was too late! "They left very early," their host explained.

"Sir, could you give me Tekle's address in Awasa?" Mark requested.

"Certainly," the man answered as he wrote it for him.

Wondering how the Wendells got his post office box number, Tekle first read the warm, friendly letter and Christian greetings. Then he took a booklet from the envelope called *Baptism in Jesus' Name* by Michael Trapasso. (For the author's account of how God directed the writing of this pamphlet, see the appendix.)

As Tekle read the title, it seemed his heart leaped within him and shattered. Jesus stood before him in soft

Baptism in the Name

Unseen Hands

glowing light with extended arms. His body opened as a delicate, translucent cloak, and Tekle stepped inside. The body of Jesus closed around him in a moment of exquisite bliss.

Tekle stood trembling as the vision faded. What does this mean? he wondered. After all my service to Christ, am I still outside? Am I not *in* Him? I do not understand this vision. He shook his head to clear his mind. Let me read the small book, he decided.

He read three pages of the booklet and saw that the author discussed baptism. He closed the book in disgust thinking, I have been baptized once; there is no second baptism! And what power is there in water baptism, anyway? From the vision, he had expected to read something far more profound than a discussion of baptism. Immediately, the Spirit moved heavily in his heart and compelled him to take his Bible and concordance and go on his knees to study the importance of water in the Bible and the types and shadows of baptism.

God led him through His Word and opened his understanding with compelling illumination. He wrote down four points, with relevant scriptural references:

1. Water is a life-giving force, and it is associated with the move of the Holy Spirit (Genesis 1:2; Ezekiel 47:1-12). (Water was mentioned at the time of creation and was a symbol of spiritual renewal in Ezekiel's vision.)

2. Noah and his family were saved by water, by floating in the ark (Genesis 6-7; I Peter 3:20-21).

3. God's covenant of circumcision with Abraham specified that it was "unto thee and thy seed after thee" (Genesis 17:1-14), and it operated until Christ. In the New Testament church, circumcision was replaced by baptism

Baptism in the Name

of water and Spirit (Colossians 2:11-14). Abraham's covenant removed only the foreskin; the new covenant, brought in by Jesus, puts off the whole sinful Adamic body to replace it with the body of Christ (John 1:12-14; 3:1-6; I Corinthians 15:39-50; Galatians 3:27-29; Ephesians 2:13-19; Philippians 3:20-21).

4. The crossing of the Red Sea provides a clear indication of water baptism's key role in the plan of salvation (I Corinthians 10:1-2). The crossing of the Jordan River and the water springing from the rock at Horeb are also significant in this regard.

Tekle saw clearly: a refusal to be circumcised excluded an Israelite male from God's covenant in the Old Testament, and any person who refuses to be baptized in the name of Jesus is excluded from the New Testament Church of Christ. He is not identified with the body of Jesus.

After reaching this conclusion, he opened the booklet again. This time, he read it through with joy. Everything in it agreed with his new understanding of the Scripture.

Tekle found himself in a dilemma. He had no choice but to be baptized in the name of Jesus. Would he become a stumbling block to the Christians who had confidence in him? What of the thousands he had won to Christ? Would this step confuse them? Would the judgment of God fall on him because he had become a stumbling block? He did not find immediate answers to his questions.

This disclosure from the Word moved him profoundly. He could not be silent. He dismayed his friends by harping on the subject. Several told him sharply, "Stop; I do not want to hear another word."

Erkenesh thought, I will divorce him if he persists

in this delusion.

Tekle prayed, "O Jesus, give me wisdom so that I do not offend believers by witnessing about baptism in Your name. Should I rather go to the heathen and baptize them correctly when they believe?"

The Lord's answer came with vivid haste: Anyone who rejects baptism in My name rejects Me. And you yourself must be immersed in My name. Can you not understand that the Scripture plainly declares, "Except a man be born of water and of the Spirit, he cannot enter into the kingdom of God"? Where is the sin if a person is offended by your true testimony?

God's message made Tekle leap with joy and gave him courage to declare boldly the truth revealed to him. Colossians 3:17 thrilled him: "And whatsoever ye do in word or deed, do all in the name of the Lord Jesus, giving thanks to God and the Father by him." He said, "I will practice this command for the rest of my life."

In spite of the sharp dissension between them, Tekle and Erkenesh went to the village of Sibaye in Wollayta for a service in an S.I.M. church. At the conclusion, young and old lifted their hands in worship, with most of them speaking in other tongues as the Holy Ghost moved.

Suddenly Tekle was impressed to look for a man whom Satan was trying to smother. He moved among the people and found the victim. He had buried his face in the sand to keep from screaming. When Tekle lifted him up, he gave out horrible shrieks until Tekle commanded the devil to leave him. The man had long been extremely ill. Jesus healed him and filled him with the Spirit in one operation.

Tekle and Erkenesh fasted and prayed for a con-

Baptism in the Name

ference at Shone, in Kambata District. At the same time, the elders of five S.I.M. churches in Gacheno Village had gathered to seek God. They felt inadequate to lead the churches under their care and were dissatisfied with their Christian experience. While they fasted and prayed throughout the night, one made a plea to the Lord, while the others agreed, "Send us a leader, Lord. Send us one to teach us and lead us in the right way. We need an anointed preacher tomorrow. If You do not answer by tomorrow morning, we are ready to give up. If You really hear and answer prayer, send him in the morning."

That same night, God directed Tekle and Erkenesh not to go to the conference, but to go to Gacheno early the next morning, where men were fasting and praying.

While the elders were still praying, Tekle and Erkenesh approached the church. The elders ran out to meet them joyfully, praising the Lord that He really does answer prayer. So began a mutually beneficial affinity: Tekle ministered to the churches, a Holy Ghost revival quickened them from the pulpit to the pew, and they blessed their leaders with material benefits.

Before going to Wollayta, Tekle tried to force Erkenesh to read the booklet on baptism in the name of Jesus, but she consistently refused. At Wollayta, Erkenesh continued to resist the message on baptism, and she became seriously ill. In spite of many prayers she did not improve. Before Tekle went to the market for a service, he lay the booklet on the table by her bed.

In between feverish tossing and turning, she picked it up, glanced at the title, *Baptism in Jesus' Name,* and put it back on the table without opening it. She felt the Lord telling her, Whatever bears My name is all good.

She began reading. It was not until after she finished the book that she suddenly realized, I am healed! This is a powerful message and the true baptism!

Tekle found her rejoicing and preparing dinner when he returned.

While Tekle and Erkenesh fasted and prayed at the home of Data Gareno, pastor of the church in Sabore Village, the Lord impressed them, You know My Word; you will be condemned if you do not speedily obey and be baptized in My name.

Tekle thought, Maybe we should go down to the river. I could baptize Erkenesh and she could baptize me.

The Lord impressed him again, Go to the people who sent you the booklet. They will baptize you in My name.

Tekle protested, "How can I go to missionaries to be baptized? That will make me a member of their church. You told me not to affiliate with a religious organization, nor to be snared by the money of missionaries to be a hired evangelist. Did You not tell me to wait until You reveal the right church to me?"

The answer came: This is My church that believes and teaches the gospel preached by the apostles. I have sent My church to Ethiopia with the true message. Go and be baptized.

Before Erkenesh had time to ask how, the Lord who had spoken provided the means for them to go to Addis.

The bus left them in the heart of the city; they telephoned Sister Wendell to come and get them. When they told her why they had come, she shouted, "Praise the Lord!" over and over. Brother Wendell rejoiced greatly with them as they told, step by step, the story of God's leading them to be baptized.

Baptism in the Name

Kenneth Wendell, hoping the baptism of Tekle and Erkenesh in the name of Jesus would open the doors of the Full Gospel Believers to the truth, sent word of the event to those he had met. Besides the Wendells' children—Mark, Angela, Jeanie, and Chester (Chet)—a large number of Tekle's friends gathered on the bank of the Akaki River on October 14, 1969. Just before entering the water, Tekle read John 8:31-32, and declared boldly, "Baptism in the name of Jesus is the true baptism and will set me free. This is God's glorious liberty."

After Brother Wendell baptized them, Tekle and Erkenesh fell on the sand in their wet clothes to pray. They fully expected to weep and groan in the Spirit as they formerly did in prayer; instead, a spirit of rejoicing came from the depths of their souls and a litany of praise poured from their lips.

Erkenesh wondered aloud to Sister Wendell, "Is it right to feel so happy and free? What has happened to the burdened, grieving kind of prayer that I usually pray?"

"You have been baptized in the name of Jesus for the remission of your sins. They are forever gone and you *are* free," Sister Wendell replied. "Rejoice!"

Unseen Hands

A country church.

8

Beacons

From a summit it is possible to glance down into the valley and identify flickering lights along the road just traveled. Although they may not shine with full radiance, and although they may appear insignificant at the time, yet they steadfastly indicate the upward path. "Line upon line; here a little, and there a little" (Isaiah 28:13). Isaiah foretold the gradual advancement of spiritual knowledge. A small glimmer of light sparked in a hungry heart, and it passed from that heart to another heart yearning for reality.

Void of evangelism, the Orthodox (Coptic) church of Ethiopia existed in rigid insulation in the late nineteenth century. The hierarchy accepted a translation of the Psalms called Dawit, which was handwritten on parchment and which few could afford to own. They considered the Scriptures printed on paper to be heretical. The brave who dared to read the written Word in those days suffered merciless persecution, loss of personal property, excommunication, and denial of all religious rites, including church burial.

Fully aware of the hazard, Gebre-Ewostateos obtained a copy of the New Testament from Evangelical translators and studied it joyfully. Both of his parents were descended from a long line of respected priests and longed for their son to succeed his father as head of the village church. When they discovered him reading the forbidden book, they stomped it irretrievably in the mud.

He protested, "This is God's Word!"

His father angrily retorted, "There is no Word of God besides Dawit."

Gebre-Ewostateos obtained another Bible from the Evangelical Mission in 1890. His mother threw it in the fire, but she could not end his friendship with men who encouraged him to examine the traditions of the church in light of the Scriptures. A venerable monk, Abba Gebre-Egziabher, inspired him by denouncing the unscriptural worship of Mary, the worship of angels, and the masses said for the dead. His approval of the monk's dissension cost Gebre-Ewostateos his position as priest in 1891 and the allowance that came with the title.

With hard-to-understand logic, church leaders recycled him as an evangelist, a downgraded position in their thinking. He assisted a priest named Selomon for a time and built a life-long friendship, and they shared a burning zeal for evangelism. A Swedish missionary society then asked Gebre-Ewostateos to work as a translator. By the end of 1896, he had produced the four Gospels, Genesis to the books of Samuel, a reader, and a Bible history in Tigrinya. His expertise in that language and his frequent evangelistic efforts did not satisfy his intense burden for the Oromo people that motivated him to learn their language secretly. Gumesh, his wife, felt the same call, and against fierce objections and with much hardship, they took their small daughter Wolete-Hiyot and went to fulfill a missionary call to the Oromos.

The friends of Gebre-Ewostateos knew that he prepared his sermons by spending long hours in the wilderness, weeping in prayer. He brought the church he established into a closer relationship to God and dispensed with many old traditions that were not founded on the Bible. He endured many tribulations and painful persecutions. He innovated a highly beneficial custom of inviting believers to his home for coffee and messages from the Word of God after the formal early morning service. He had more liberty in his home than in the church. He boldly opposed the evils of his day, from vain religious rituals to slavery. His oldest daughter remembered how he carefully saved his money to buy slaves, free them, and give them a new start in life.

One day, his old friend Gebre-Egziabher sat on his customary three-legged stool at Michael's Church and taught against error, angering his colleagues. They incited a religious mob by screaming, "This man is anti-Mary!" They dragged him from the church yard with the command, "Stone the heretic!"

One lady, in a dilemma between pity and fear, threw a leaf. The monk came to the home of Gebre-Ewostateos with blood streaming down his face and laughed about his "leaf blessing"; it brought no blood!

Her heart touched by his plight, Salome, the second daughter of Gebre-Ewostateos, looked up to heaven exclaiming, "God avenge you of these evil men!"

"My child, do not speak as a foolish one," the monk

answered. "My Lord was beaten by men who did not know Him. If they had known who He was, they would not have crucified Him. I will say as my Lord did, 'Father, forgive them for they know not what they do.'"

The Orthodox clergy then had Gebre-Egziabher thrown into prison with common criminals. Outraged, the empress Zewditu sent an official to release him. He refused freedom, declaring, "I have found a needy field where I can preach to hungry souls." He finally agreed to leave jail on the condition that he would be allowed to return and minister whenever he chose.

The monk remained a consistent thorn in the flesh to orthodoxy until his death at the venerable age of 120.

Salome, the girl who grieved over the monk's stoning, grew up with a heart tender toward God. She married a man name Asfaw, and they lived in Addis Ababa with their six children—two sons, Tewodros and Yohannes; and four daughters, Marta, Sophia, Aster, and Genet—all of whom serve God today.

One day Salome saw an old, white man with a long, snowy beard circling their property while he called out something. She could only understand one word he said: "Asfaw" (her husband's name). Immobile from wonder and surprise, she watched as he found a small hole in the back fence and crawled through, found a chair in the yard, and sat down. When Salome came to speak to him, he asked her name. He ignored her answer, "Salome," and said, "You are Lisa. My name is Alfred David. I am a servant of Jesus Christ, who is the one true God. He spoke to me in my own country of Holland and told me to come to Ethiopia and tell the people of this land who He is and that He wants to live in their hearts in the power of the

Holy Ghost, speaking in other tongues. Jesus told me to come to Asfaw's house. It has taken me a long time, nearly two years, to walk from Egypt."

Salome understood very little that he said in a mixture of Dutch, Arabic, Oromo, and German, with a smattering of English, but in the gracious Ethiopian manner of hospitality she motioned him to enter the house. Her husband spoke some German and could communicate with him in a small way.

Instinctively, they felt that God had sent him, and they prepared a small room for him off a porch at the front of their house. Though he never learned to speak Amharic properly, he quickly learned to read the Bible in Amharic, and often used the Scriptures to explain what he struggled to say.

At one point the authorities wanted to deport him, but Salome's husband pleaded his cause and promised to take care of him.

He often scolded the Ethiopians for believing in a trinity of gods. "The Moslems are wiser than you," he would declare. "At least they know that there is only one God."

When called to eat and asked to say grace, he often became lost in the Spirit, worshiping the Lord in other tongues. The family would hesitantly begin to eat and finish the meal and be gone long before he came to himself. Sometimes he knelt on the grass for hours, praising God, looking up to heaven at intervals and shouting, "Spirit of God, welcome!"

Frequently he interrupted the children at play with an open Bible. "This is God's Word; read here and here." Strangely, the children understood him better than the adults. They shouted, marched, danced, and praised God without the faintest notion of why. They simply followed his direction. Early in his stay the family gave him the name Paulus and soon forgot his real name.

After the Italian invasion in 1936, he said, "Lisa, prepare my breakfast. My Father told me the Italians will take me to a place where I can do my work."

"Let it not happen," she answered, while she complied with his request. Only a few yards down the road, Italian police stopped him and, being suspicious of his answers to their questions, committed him to a jail in Dire Dowa. He returned several months later to a warm welcome.

"How did you get out of prison?" Asfaw's family asked.

He did not appreciate his release. "That was the perfect place for my work," he answered with disgust, "but the authorities said, 'Send this man away; we cannot stand his loud prayers,' so they sent me back."

One day Salome saw her eccentric guest staggering toward the house, holding onto the fence and sometimes falling.

Oh, he's drunk, she thought, and hurried to help him. When she reached him she saw that he trembled violently. No, he's not drunk, she realized, he's having a stroke or a heart attack. I must get him to the hospital.

He resisted going and kept repeating, "I'm not sick, praise God, hallelujah. I'm not sick."

A Dutch nurse at the hospital explained to Salome, "He is not sick; the power of God is on him. The Lord has made him wonderful promises. He said, 'The name of Jesus will rise over Ethiopia mightier than the sun.'"

When Salome took him home, he ran up and down the yard praising the Lord at the top of his voice for the remainder of the day.

He always fasted forty days once a year at Easter. At the close of one fast, he came out of his room leaping. Those who beheld him in amazement later testified that the Spirit held him a yard above the floor while he prophesied, "A mighty revival will sweep across Ethiopia. Great miracles will be done in the name of Jesus. The Holy Ghost will be poured upon you, my friends."

He turned to Ayele, Marta's teenage son. "You, my son, will be filled with the Spirit and will become a preacher of the gospel."

Ayele turned away, not pleased with the prophecy concerning him.

Slowly, Paulus settled to the floor and in a different tone said, "I've had a call from my Father. He said that I am tired and have worked enough; He will take me home."

The younger children cried and begged him not to go. He looked slowly around the room at his friends and said softly, "My blood will flow to pay my dues for the revival."

When he went to stay with another family that he often visited, no one at Asfaw's house realized that he would not return. He asked a friend to buy him some funeral clothes. She refused, saying, "No, I will not give you up."

As Paulus walked through town on Christmas day, a car struck him. Ayele heard the cry, "Accident! There's been an accident!" He ran to the scene, and there lay the old Dutchman dead in the road. His blood trickled slowly toward the gutter.

The old man's prophecy that he would be a preacher burned uncomfortably in Ayele's mind. He turned away, muttering, "Why did I go and look? It is stupid to be drawn by curiosity to view someone's misfortune."

Along with the rest of Asfaw's family, Ayele grieved sorely over the Dutchman's passing, and nothing he did would erase the words that he heard or the blood that he saw in the street.

Several years later his surrender to God brought him peace as Tekle prayed with him in the old Dutchman's prayer room and God filled him with the Holy Ghost.

Paulus spent thirty-three years in and out of Asfaw's house. Although he saw no results of his witness during his lifetime, time would reveal his influence for good on members of that household.

The memory of the old Dutchman lingers as a beacon, an out-of-the-ordinary finger, that pointed toward a sweeping deluge of God's Holy Spirit on a thirsty land.

Tekle and Erkenesh.

9

The Lord Said Go

"Tekle and his wife allowed a new missionary to baptize them in a strange manner. Tekle even read from John and declared that this new baptism would set him free." The Full Gospel Believers hurried to share the startling news with their elders. Confused and disturbed, they chose a reputable leader to investigate the matter.

He came to the Wendells' service that Sunday night and heard both Tekle and Erkenesh witness of the overwhelming joy that came to them after baptism in the name of Jesus.

On his return, the leader's report triggered a furious discussion after which the presiding elder summarized their feelings: "We esteemed Brother Teklemariam highly and thought him to be a great man of God—his messages have touched the hearts of thousands—but now he has become a heretic. We must make plans to discredit him, else his wide influence will deceive many into following his error."

They all agreed.

Unseen Hands

Filled with joy and peace, the newly baptized couple gave themselves to fasting and prayer for the next four days before the Wendells took them back to Awasa. They had no idea of the decision made against them nor that the name of Jesus would bring acute division between them and a host of friends. An anointed service at Awasa brought Tekle's family to the truth, and Brother Wendell baptized Tekle's mother and two sisters as well as Erkenesh's sister and her husband before he returned to Addis the next day.

Infinite wisdom directed Tekle and Erkenesh to a town 450 kilometers away (two days' bus ride). Tekle's mother, two sisters, and a nephew looked to him for support. He explained to them, "God is sending us to Negele-Borana. I am compelled to use the bit of money reserved for food to pay our fare on the bus."

"Many of us wonder," his troubled mother sighed, "why both of you do not get a job and make a living for us."

"I do not understand God's ways," Tekle explained gently, "but I must be obedient. We have no money for food on the journey, nor for our living expenses at Negele, nor for the return trip home. Still, we must believe that Jesus knows and that He will provide for you who remain here, and for us as we go."

Tekle and Erkenesh took one hundred Bibles with them to sell for the Philadelphia Pentecostal Church of Awasa. They reached Negele on October 22, 1969, and the Lord directed them to ask for lodging at the Norwegian Lutheran Mission. Reluctantly, those in charge allotted them a small room.

Before time for the Saturday evening worship, Tekle

The Lord Said Go

humbly asked permission to preach. The missionaries uneasily agreed after a long discussion.

Tekle and Erkenesh sang a duet, then Erkenesh testified of the joyful changes in her life after she received her personal Pentecost. Tekle read from the second chapter of Acts about the outpouring of the Holy Ghost and said, "Let us pray."

Instantly, a great wave of God's presence swept across the auditorium. Everyone fell on his knees, some prostrate upon the floor. Some wept and groaned in repentance while others rejoiced. After a while, those who were weeping began to praise the Lord and dance, and seventy of them began to speak fluently in strange languages. About this time the Ethiopian elders and the missionaries rushed out of the hall, evidently preferring to watch the unusual happening through the window. About half the congregation received a mighty filling of the Holy Ghost.

"I did not get to bring the message God gave me last night. I would like to give it tonight, if you will kindly give your permission." Tekle's respectful humility changed the disapproval the frowning leaders had planned to express, and they ungraciously gave him another chance.

He had hardly reached the pulpit when the Spirit came as a powerful wind and took control of the worshipers. All who were not filled with the Spirit in the Saturday night service and who desired to be filled received their own experience with exuberant shouts of joy and dancing. The elders and the missionaries hurried angrily to their usual place outside to watch through the windows.

"I haven't preached yet; I need to finish one sermon

at least." Tekle's plea gained the pulpit for him the third time, the next night. The Lord allowed him to preach that time, and heavenly blessings rained on the hearers afterwards.

Agitated missionaries and elders confronted him after the service. "You are bringing division in our church. These who claim to have received the Holy Ghost, speaking in other tongues, stand against those who do not think it is necessary. You cannot preach here again, and you must vacate at once the room we gave you. We beg you to leave our town and never return."

Tekle and Erkenesh had fasted two days before they came to Negele. With no offer of food at the mission, they continued to fast, but they had to find shelter for the night. (Men of this area proved their masculinity by either castrating or killing strange men.)

With darkness closing in upon them, they knelt beside their bundle of belongings on the roadside and cried to the Lord for help. He directed them to ask for a room at the best hotel in town and assured them that money for the bill would come in time.

Contrary to prevailing custom, the host gave them a room without asking for payment in advance. Neither did he pound on the door of their second floor room each evening at six o'clock demanding his fee for their staying another night. They lay on the floor praying and seeking God's face for five nights and four days, still fasting.

"Since we can't pay, we will not sleep on the bed," Tekle said.

At night they wrestled with the powers of darkness that controlled the town, which appeared to them at times as giants armed with fiery spears. Often it seemed that they would be blinded and overcome, but they fought the evil spirits with the name of Jesus. Victory came, bringing new courage and boldness to preach the gospel with power.

A sudden, loud knock on the door made Tekle and Erkenesh tremble; they thought their host had come to collect the overdue fees. A sergeant whom God had filled with His Spirit during the services stood before them. "Oh!" he exclaimed happily. "I am so glad to find you. I've looked for you all over town. Here is forty-nine birr in tithes that the Lord told me to give to you."

Thankfully, Tekle paid for their room, and they broke their long fast. The sergeant spread the word that he had found them.

The same day a couple invited them to teach the Word to a group of people gathered in the army camp. On entering the room, as Tekle and Erkenesh greeted each one with a handshake, all of them reacted as though they had touched a live electric wire.

They taught continuously for two days. Seven were delivered from demon possession, and eleven more received the Holy Spirit. The community rose against them on the third day; military police arrested their host, fined him, and put him in jail for three days.

After a week in Negele the Lord instructed Tekle to return to Awasa and en route to be a witness in the towns He would show him.

Tekle found himself in a familiar predicament, with no money for transportation or for lodging in the towns that they would visit on the way.

The Lord answered their desperate prayer by telling them to use the 250 birr from the sale of Bibles. He assured them that when they got to Awasa the exact amount of money would be waiting for them to pay their debt.

On the way home they preached in Arekello, Wadera, Kibre-Mengist and Yirga-Alem. At the close of a well-attended market meeting in Wadera, a man came to Tekle and Erkenesh with this incredible story:

"Immediately after I married my first wife, a demon in her said that I would die if I touched her and if I did not play the drums while she danced every night until both of us became totally exhausted.

"Frustrated, I decided to take a second wife and found her possessed of a similar demon. Without peace or fulfillment, I spend my evenings playing the drums for these women to dance. How can I be set free from the threat of death and demonic bondage?"

Tekle and Erkenesh helped the man to find the liberty of full salvation and sent him home armed with the mighty name of Jesus.

He returned joyfully. "I hurried home and declared, 'I believe in Jesus, the mighty God who created heaven and earth. You, Satan, are a deceiver and I command you in the name of Jesus to come out of these women and to leave my house forever.' Jesus delivered them; now, what must I do?"

"Keep your first wife," Tekle advised, "and separate from the second one. The Word of God does not allow you to have two wives."

When the man had testified with great joy of how Jesus brought peace to his house, another man asked permission to speak.

"The god of my forefathers has not been the Jesus

you preach, but he has been a huge tree in my village. Yesterday morning as I worshiped my ancestral god, he told me that if I did not slaughter my four cows as a sacrifice to him that he would kill all of my children. I am a cattle-raising nomad, and we live from the milk of the cows. My cows have recently calved; if I kill them, we will surely die of hunger. Would your God save me and my family if I believe in Him? Can you guarantee that your Jesus will deliver me from this critical situation?"

"Jesus will certainly set you free from this bondage," Tekle answered firmly. "He is omnipotent, omnipresent and omniscient; all power in heaven and in earth is in His all-powerful name, Jesus. Satan is speaking to you from that tree."

Tekle then laid hands on him and prayed that he would be delivered and would receive the power of God. Through the Word this man realized the depth of the bondage that had held him. Today, he and his family rejoice in the liberty of life in Christ.

Abebech, one of the ladies filled with the Spirit at Negele, came to Wadera carrying her desperately ill child on her back. In the name of Jesus, Tekle and Erkenesh laid their hands on the almost lifeless body, and in a few minutes the child recovered completely. This lady is an earnest soul winner in the strong church the Lord established at Negele.

At Kibre-Menguist, Tekle preached to twenty-five thousand people in the market. The following morning a priest invited him to speak at a Coptic church, and the Holy Spirit melted the hearts of the listeners. They wept in repentance.

An opportunity came to speak to high school students.

Unseen Hands

Fifteen of them followed Tekle and Erkenesh to their hotel room. "Pray for us; we want the Holy Ghost," they entreated.

Several of them had received their desire when the hotel owner beat on the door. "Stop making this awful noise!" he yelled.

They moved the prayer meeting to a nearby forest and prayed until every student was mightily filled with the Spirit.

Tekle and Erkenesh committed the new believers to the Lord who knows how to keep and direct babes in Christ, and they went on to Yirga-Alem. At Negele they had met Mrs. Sunyiva, a Norwegian missionary and psychologist who lived in Yirga-Alem. Though she rejected the apostolic message, she entertained the travelers kindly in her home for two days. Tekle preached fervently, but they saw no results. After they left eighty high school students responded belatedly to the message, began to seek God, received the Holy Ghost, and were baptized later.

"You will not believe what happened!" Tekle's mother rejoiced, when they reached Awasa again. "Just after you left for Negele, a man came from Harar looking for you—you know that is eight hundred kilometers from here. He would not tell us his name, and we did not tell him of our need; he brought us 220 pounds of teff and gave me forty birr for the household."

"God sent an angel to supply your needs!" Tekle and Erkenesh agreed. Passing years have strengthened that conviction, for that man has not been seen since.

A message from the bank sent Tekle to inquire. He found that Sister Sophia Asfaw had sent him 250 birr.

The Lord Said Go

He took it immediately to the Philadelphia Church to pay the Bible money they had borrowed on the Lord's instruction. The preacher gave him fifty birr for his trouble.

Some of those filled with the Holy Ghost at the Norwegian Lutheran Mission. Two are now strong preachers and leaders in the A.C.E.

Unseen Hands

Brother Wendell baptizing Tekle's mother and two sisters.

Brother Wendell just after the Bible lesson that convinced Tekle's family to be baptized in Jesus' name.

10

Rejection

As a highly respected nondenominational preacher, Tekle enjoyed the esteem of many religious groups; each one wanted him to become a member of its church or mission. After his baptism in the name of Jesus, he became the target of malicious opposition.

Trying to persude him to renounce his baptism, a committee of leading ministers from the Full Gospel Believers' Fellowship came to reason with him. When the mission failed, they returned to Addis to spread ridiculous rumors about Tekle and Erkenesh.

Prophecies against Tekle and his family became the special feature of all-night prayer sessions. On August 16, 1970, God blessed Tekle and Erkenesh with a daughter. They named her Mehret, meaning mercy. One widely told prophecy sent a drove of travelers to Awasa to see God's judgment. The prophet said that Mehret, who was only a few months old, had been born with withered arms and legs. Erkenesh patiently displayed her perfect, lovely, and lively daughter to all visitors, who examined her carefully and returned home ashamed.

Salome, Marta, and Sophia noticed how thin Erkenesh appeared and learned that in her zeal for God she had fasted four days a week for eight months of her pregnancy. They urged her to eat for the sake of her baby's nourishment. Visitors to Awasa saw more of a miracle than they realized.

Tekle attended a conference at the Philadelphia Church. In his sermon the preacher declared that Tekle had a demon which could only be cast out by the blood of a lamb, referring to Old Testament passages that describe a lamb's blood shed as a sacrifice.

Tekle raised his hand for permission to speak. "I have a question. . ."

On hearing his voice, the whole crowd began shouting, "Blood! Blood!"

When nothing happened, the preacher said, "This man is possessed of a very stubborn demon who refuses to come out."

On another day at the conference, one of their prophets, a huge, tall man, came toward him trembling, with outstretched arms and palms turned sideways. "You who sow tares among my people, I will cut you in half!" he denounced, as he hit Tekle on the head with all his might.

Tekle swayed, nearly fainting, but the Lord strengthened him.

An evangelist sitting nearby began to wail loudly.

"Why are you crying?" Tekle asked.

"Because God is going to cut you in two," he answered.

"God will not cut me in two," Tekle replied. "I suffered from the blow on the head that your so-called prophet gave me, but my God is not involved in such ridiculous games."

Opposition and wild predictions continued; however, month followed month and none of the dire things foretold for Tekle happened. Sadly, many of those who prophesied against him suffered the fate they predicted for him, and others backslid. The furor hindered revival. A backlash of rumors caused even the faithful to neglect their financial responsibility to God's work. Without tithe-payers Tekle and Erkenesh suffered acute need.

The Lord answered their cry for help in an unusual way: Mrs. Sunyiva from Yirga-Alem drove seventy-five kilometers to Awasa to bring them two hundred birr. "The Lord has ordered me to give you this amount every month."

She always came after dark, parked her car several blocks away, and walked to their house—a secretive raven who came regularly. Two years later, she developed cancer and returned to her native Norway to end her days. By the time her support ended, a number had been baptized in the name of Jesus and had obeyed the Bible's command to tithe.

Unseen Hands

Area conference.

Opening a new area.

11

Such as Should be Saved

With a desire to serve the Lord, Salome, the daughter of Gebre-Ewostateos, became a Lutheran and sent her children to Sunday school. The small exposure to the Scriptures did not spare them the emptiness of heart that drives human beings to despair. While very young, her son Yohannes became an alcoholic; neither noble birth nor wealth could restore his mind and health.

Salome's daughter Sophia became a beauty queen, made a prestigious marriage, and suffered from depression severe enough to make her consider suicide. During this time of mental torment that psychiatrists could not alleviate, she had a strange dream. She saw a woman with beautiful, long hair who spoke in a language that Sophia could not understand. An Ethiopian man in the dream interpreted her words: "Can you not see that this is the true religion?"

Just before the Ethiopian Easter in 1968, a nephew

Unseen Hands

that Salome had partly raised asked the family to go with him to the Finnish Pentecostal Mission. "These people definitely have more of God. A lady named Ruth, a missionary en route to India, will be speaking for a few days. Please come and hear her."

Sophia refused to go, but Salome and her daughters Marta and Aster accepted his invitation. As the service progressed, Salome trembled at the touch of the Spirit.

"She is having a stroke!" Marta thought and took her home.

Salome insisted on going again the next night, and Sophia, becoming curious, followed them. That night Ruth interpreted a message in tongues that was given by a poor man in worn, patched trousers. He predicted revolution and much bloodshed ahead. A deep hunger for the Holy Ghost filled this family, and they sought without receiving for two nights.

In the next meeting, a demon-possessed Coptic priest who was sent to spy on the service fell screaming to the floor. Salome's family watched Tekle and other leaders rebuke the evil spirits, who immediately vacated that abode, making room for God's Spirit to fill the man. This victory as well as Tekle's worship and playing of the accordion touched Sophia's heart, and she impulsively invited all of them to her house for refreshments.

Marta received the Holy Spirit first, followed by the others, with Sophia being the last one to receive the promised gift.

Sophia's heart overflowed with the fresh sweetness of God's Spirit, and this moved her to witness to the employees and neighbors at her dairy at Kuriftu, ten kilometers from Nazareth.

During the 1950's Salome had a shop at Nazareth, and there she had met Mamma Elfenesh, the most feared and renowned witch in Ethiopia. Royalty, state officials, nobility, and ordinary folk alike came to this woman for counsel, for charms to overcome real and imaginary enigmas, for foretelling the future, and for vengeance on enemies.

Salome's compassionate heart perceived her as a lonely, desperately unhappy old lady who needed a friend. Salome became her friend, treated her with kindness and consideration, and ignored her profession. Elfenesh, in turn, confided in Salome.

Her family told the following story concerning the supposed source of her spiritual powers. Her father, esteemed as a war hero and a hunter, killed a demon-possessed deer one day. The demon entered him, making him violently ill. Elfenesh, the child of his sickness, began making true predictions at the age of three. At the age of seven, Elfenesh was picked up from her mother's home by a demonic whirlwind and was carried to remote mountains. Satan kept her and trained her until the same whirlwind deposited her at her widowed mother's door seven years later.

She operated as a powerful sorceress from the age of fourteen and received many gifts from her clients, though Satan never allowed her to accumulate anything. She trained many witches; one of them, Mistress Arussi, became famous beyond the borders of Ethiopia.

Burning with zeal after the Holy Ghost came, Salome told Sophia, "I feel that we should fast and pray for Elfenesh; she is over fifty years old and has never known peace or happiness." While they sought God for Mamma

Elfenesh, she came to tell Salome about a vision she had.

"I saw yoked oxen fly out of my house and fly toward the east. I think I am going to be delivered. If your Jesus will save me from my cruel master," the trembling woman wept, "I will serve Him until I die, and I will destroy all the artifacts of my trade."

Tekle went with Salome and Sophia to Elfenesh's house, and on her confession that she wanted deliverance, they prayed and rebuked the devil in the name of Jesus. Forty screaming demon leaders came out of her, claiming that a thousand evil spirits worked under each of them. By the unfathomable mercy of God, as all of these agents of Satan moved out the precious Holy Ghost moved in, bringing peace and joy beyond words.

Immediately she burned the elaborate gowns and the implements that she had used while offering sacrifices to Satan. She made a pilgrimage to every home and palace of her clients, lowly and great, and with or without their permission, she burned or threw into the toilet all the fetishes and charms that she had previously given them. The common report was that she had lost her mind. She rejoiced that she had found it at last!

Elfenesh witnessed to everyone with brimming joy and assurance, and she especially loved to attend services in the chapel that Sophia built. Brother Wolde-Giorgis Sisay came during that time to serve as pastor of the sizeable, growing flock.

Salome, her three daughters, and her sister Woletehiwot rejoiced in the liberty of the Holy Ghost. They spent many hours studying the Word and praying together. One day they felt impressed of the Lord that something was not right, that something was missing in their experience.

Such as Should Be Saved

They cried in anguished conviction, "O Lord, what do we lack?" They decided to go to Sophia's farm at Kuriftu for a time of prayer and fasting. Mamma Elfenesh accompanied them.

The answer came in one word: baptism.

Several days passed in earnest prayer and detailed study on baptism before Woletehiwot shared a new scriptural understanding with her family. "We are following the tradition of men and we fear people. The word teaches immersion so we are not baptized right by sprinkling."

While the others felt hesitant and fearful, Mamma Elfenesh said, "If it is my Lord's command, I will not only be baptized in water, but even in fire."

On their return, they went to the Finnish Pentecostal church for a communion service. The missionary in charge asked, "Have you been baptized?" When they answered no, he wanted to baptize them in the titles. They felt compelled to refuse, and they never returned.

Though Tekle and Erkenesh felt responsibility for the work in Awasa, the Lord impressed them to go to Addis and assist the Wendells for a time. They invited their friends Solomon and Teshome to discuss the Scriptures at Brother Wendell's house. They brought along Teshome's friend Amare. Later when they went to the river to baptize the three men, Brother Wendell insisted that Tekle do the baptizing, even though he stood in the water with them.

Tekle and Erkenesh took turns holding services in the homes of Salome and her children. God revealed the truth to them, and Tekle baptized all of them in the Akaki River.

When Sophia came to visit Tekle and Erkenesh at the Wendells' house, Bobbye Wendell's first sight of Sophia brought shock. Obviously moved, Sister Wendell told her of a vision she had had in America, long before she came to Ethiopia. "I saw a lovely Ethiopian lady like you, wearing a traditional dress."

Just as moved, Sophia recognized Sister Wendell as the woman with beautiful, long hair that she had seen in a vision. She ran to her and kissed her.

"That is what you did in my vision," Sister Wendell said. The Wendells met the rest of Salome's family when they came to the church services.

Three years after her conversion, Elfenesh became ill, and the Lord told her He would take her home. A young Mennonite girl who loved Elfenesh insisted that she go to the hospital. She disregarded her protests, saying, "The Lord said it is time for me to go to my everlasting home. I don't need the hospital."

Elfenesh died in the hospital a few days later. At the funeral, which was attended by thousands of people, her young friend, Yechale-Yansash, sobbed in grief. Suddenly, the angel of the Lord pulled her aside and showed her two beautiful angels carrying the soul of Mamma Elfenesh to heaven. He said, "Your friend is going to her mansion in the presence of Jesus; do not grieve for her, but grieve for yourself."

The young lady, though she did not come to the Lord, told everyone present of her vision. Elfenesh left a blessed legacy to those she won with her testimony of deliverance.

While Salome's son wandered drunk up and down the city's streets, a car hit him. His mother and his sisters shared the sweet story of salvation with him during his recovery in the hospital.

Afterwards, he came to tell them about a strange dream: "Two invisible men held me as they forced me to climb a high ladder to the top of a skyscraper. They made me look down and said, 'If you turn back from now on, that's where you will land.'"

Deeply moved, he continued, "Do you think Jesus will deliver me?"

They assured him that He would. They took him to Tekle and Erkenesh for prayer, and the Lord restored his mind. They gave him a copy of Tekle's book, *Divine Power*, and he learned that heartfelt repentance would cancel the addiction of sin. Tekle baptized Yohannes; three of Marta's children, Brook, Samuel, and Wondossen; Sophia's two, Samson and Suzy; and another young lady in the Akaki River. By obedience, the outcast for thirty years received deliverance and became a new creation in Christ. This caused several officials related to the Asfaws to gain new respect for the gospel.

The government's permission for the Wendells to remain in the country depended on their activity in some type of social or educational services. They felt led to begin their work among the lepers. They built the Medhane-Alem Rehabilitation Center in the northern part of the city, across the road from the French Embassy. Brother Wendell built looms, and he taught the lepers, according to their various conditions and abilities, to weave carpets, build chairs, or make small wooden articles.

The workrooms surrounded a chapel where the workers gathered regularly for prayer and Bible study. Moved with compassion and sincerity, the Wendells brought lepers from their abode in the cemetery; however, the lepers, whose very existence from ancient times had depended on begging, developed a shrewd eye for the benefits that they hoped to receive in exchange for listening and praying. God's unfathomable mercy still brought healing to some of them and improvement to others.

None of the lepers had been baptized by the end of 1969. One Sunday, Tekle brought Salome and her family to the chapel, not knowing that Brother Wendell had designated it as a clean-up day. The nobility had brought some of their peers with them, hoping that they would benefit by the sermon they would hear. Instead, the Wendells, with commendable humility, led in the necessary cleaning of the premises, and the high-born followed their example. The visitors did not return, but Salome's family, having a deep hunger for God and the truth, came to stay with the church regardless of the lepers and their offensive odor. It is difficult for an outsider to comprehend the vast cultural taboos that love surmounted that day.

Early in 1970, Tekle and Erkenesh returned to revival blessings in Awasa. Haylu Wolde-Tsadik served as president of the Luthern Southern Synod for many years and had long been a helpful friend to Tekle. This man came to the knowledge of the truth and gave his friend the privilege of baptizing him in the name of Jesus. Haylu's stand cost him everything he had—a good salary, his home and car, and the favor of co-workers and family. He became deathly ill at a meal served while angry church officials questioned him, and he still suffers from the effects of whatever caused the illness. This did not turn him away from the truth he received.

Wolde-Girogis Sisay received the Holy Ghost while attending the Lutheran seminary. Eight trinitarian pastors—Asha Ashango, an Adventist, Dejana Segu,

Such as Should Be Saved

Mokonnen Lodamo, Data Gareno, Debissa Halchaye, Alaro Sanna, Haile Sanamo, and Abba Dama Tuleray—and four other fine men—Ashenafi Andarge, Samuel Jajerso, Birhanu Mena and Mengistu Meskele—took their stand for truth in 1970. All of these men are dedicated leaders and preachers in the Apostolic Church of Ethiopia.

"Take the truth to the churches that were formerly under your supervision," the Lord directed Tekle. He decided to start with the village of Sivay in Wollayta District. Over seventy of Pastor Alaro's members had received the Holy Ghost in earlier services Tekle held there. Over the evening meal, Tekle shared with Alaro the scriptural truth of baptism in the name of Jesus.

Alaro jumped from the table in anger. "If you were not my friend, I would kick you out of my house right now. Since there is no lodging available, you may spend the night, but I will ask you to leave early in the morning." He stormed out of the room without finishing the meal.

A tremendous light filled his room and awakened Alaro in the night. A majestic angel stood by him, and he fell to the floor trembling.

"Do not resist the life-giving message you heard from Tekle," the angel said, "and do not be an obstacle to those who desire to hear the Word."

Alaro lay on the floor weeping until dawn. He came to Tekle's room with a broken spirit and asked forgiveness for his outburst at supper. After he told of his vision, he said, "Now, please teach me the truth."

Tekle taught him and the church and baptized the adult members in the name of Jesus.

Alaro accompanied Tekle to Sabore, Gatcheno, and Offare. A group of preachers gathered at Debissa's house to hear Tekle's message. Although he did not express his feelings, Debissa felt highly offended by Tekle's words.

Alaro discerned his feelings and rose to admonish, "My fellow men, do not err. The Lord is speaking to you through this man. The Lord warned me with a vision that this is Bible truth. Do not hesitate to accept it."

Debissa remained unconvinced until a vision came to him that night. He related it the next day.

"I stood before a deep lake. Tekle and Jesus came over the water and Tekle immersed me, calling on the name of Jesus. When I came out of the water, I found myself clothed in pure white from head to toe."

Tekle sprang to his feet and explained that at baptism they would put on the pure, sinless body of Christ and their sins would be washed away. The Lord again confirmed His Word miraculously, and four churches and their pastors obeyed the Word.

In Kambata District three more churches received the Jesus Name message, along with their pastors, Haile Sanamo, Abba Dama, and Mokonnen Lodamo.

On his return to Awasa, Tekle happily reported by telephone to Brother Wendell what God had wrought. He came and visited all of the churches with Tekle and gave them assistance where feasible.

Later, the Lord told Brother Wendell to preach at Sivay and to pray for a sick man there. After he brought the Word, Brother Wendell asked, "Who is sick?"

A man with elephantiasis, evident by a horribly swollen, infected leg, hobbled to the front of the church. He received instant healing when Brother Wendell and Tekle prayed for him.

The churches of Sabore, Offare, and Gatcheno came

Such as Should Be Saved

together for a blessed conference that encouraged everyone.

By the end of 1970, sixteen churches and their pastors rejoiced in the apostolic message. Two hundred twelve had been baptized in the name of Jesus and filled with the Holy Ghost. The leaders foresaw a great future for the work in Ethiopia.

Lady testifying was healed after many years of serious illness.

Unseen Hands

Tekle, Sophia, Bobbye Wendell and Sister Elfenesh, converted witch doctor, with uplifted hands.

Tekle, Debissa and Dawit. An angel told Debissa to receive biblical baptism in Jesus' name.

Beginning of the work in Kambata District.

12

Opposition from Within and Without

"Get rid of the Pentecostals or I will resign! Even Moslems are better than Pentecostals," the pope of the Ethiopian Coptic Church, the highest religious authority in the land, threatened Emperor Haile Selasse early in 1970. The Coptic church at that time controlled one third of the land and made serfs of many citizens. The religious hierarchy felt threatened by the Pentecostals, who had found a spiritual experience that freed them from the customary abject obeisance. The emperor's allegiance to the state church demanded action, so he began a sweeping anti-Pentecostal campaign involving both the police and the militia.

On their part, those who had received the Pentecostal experience made serious mistakes. They refused all organization and firm leadership, choosing to be completely undisciplined. Many quickly fell into errors of immorality; of inconsideration of others; of unwise and openly expressed scorn for government authorities and the state church; of blatant false doctrines such as never-die, unreasonable fasting, and reading demon possession into a sneeze or the mildest pain.

A painstaking witch hunt began to ferret out Pentecostals. Receiving no consideration and according to the whim of local authorities, they were beaten, subjected to indignities, and jailed. In the midst of legal atrocities, the Wendells planted the United Pentecostal Church of Ethiopia. Government officials called Brother Wendell in and asked two things of him: "Do not accept the Pentecostal radicals into your fellowship, and change the name of your church."

He readily agreed on the first point, but felt he had to refuse the second requirement. He carefully explained, "This is the international name of our church, and I do not have authority to change it. Surely you can make a difference between our God-fearing, government-respecting church and these fanatics."

However willing the government might have been to show consideration, the persecution became an uncontrollable landslide. With the word *Pentecostal* in the middle of the church name, being identified as a Pentecostal was inevitable.

The Rehabilitation Center became an expense beyond the Wendells' means, besides being a hindrance to the growth of the church. Many objected to sharing the baptistery with those who had the dreaded disease of leprosy. Brother Wendell wisely rented a house in the western part of the city to serve the family as a residence and contrived

Opposition from Within and Without

a chapel for worship. He turned the center over to another organization. Revival came to Addis Ababa, reaching many honest-hearted people.

Not everything that happened in 1970 resulted in a blessing. Every new work has the problem of false prophets creeping in unaware. One was a former Coptic monk and secretly a witch doctor. He came to Tekle at Awasa, reporting a fictitious vision. "While I prayed in a cave a few days ago, an angel appeared and declared that baptism in the name of Jesus and the teaching of one God is true. He told me to be baptized by you and that I must go to my village and preach this gospel. He said thousands of state church members will obey the Word."

He sounded good. Tekle joyfully baptized him, and on the man's request, took him to meet Brother Wendell. The believers in Addis praised the Lord for another worker. Brother Wendell gave him money to go to Hamusi, Fitche District, believing that he went to evangelize his people. Instead, he called the village together and told them that the kindhearted missionary would build them an elementary school, a clinic, and a mill if they would donate the land. Everyone wanted the honor of giving the land and all agreed to welcome the United Pentecostal Church to their village.

The preacher sent word to Brother Wendell, "You must come. I have won the whole town to the Lord, and they have donated land for a church building." Several preachers, including Tekle, went with the Wendells, and a feast was prepared in their honor. After eating, Brother Wendell gave a strong message on the plan of salvation. Tekle and two others spoke at length on baptism. The bewildered people looked at them coldly, without comprehension. They only wanted to know how soon work would begin on the projects, how many of them would be employed, and how the village would be benefited. The day ended in mutual disappointment.

When the preacher saw his hope for easy gain about to slip away, he began to preach diligently, and seven honest souls responded to the Word and found salvation. In April 1971, Brother Wendell decided to try again in Hamusi and built a two-classroom school and chapel. He sent Worku Gebremariam and Negussie Haile to teach school and hold services.

Brother E. L. Freeman visited the site that month during construction, and Brother C. G. Weeks came for a visit shortly after completion of the building. Things went well for several months, then the same crowd that had welcomed the missionary enthusiastically turned against his efforts. Half the village became accusers and the other half gave false witness against the workers and members. Four Coptic priests manipulated the malicious trial.

Six of those judged guilty went to jail for a month. The judge claimed that Worku and Teferi Dinku, one of the believers, had been the ringleaders in the imaginary crime and sentenced them to six months of hard labor. The brothers suffered in jail, but judgment came on the priests. Three died violently in a short time and the fourth has been bedfast, suffering in agony and praying to die, for fourteen years.

Diseases have plagued the village, making many regret their action against the small church. They expelled Worku from the district when he got out of prison, and for thirteen years no preacher was allowed to set foot in

Opposition from Within and Without

Hamusi. Finally, in 1985, a church worker was able to come in, and he found six faithful saints, ostracized by family and friends and denied citizen's right. One of the number, unable to stand the pressure, had turned away from the church, and his own bull had gored him to death. Those remaining true to the Lord have not suffered from either drought or pestilence, though surrounding neighbors have lost crops and cattle to both.

Teferi Dinku came out of prison with victory, but faced another trial when his wife, Fitale Debela, died in great agony. Allowing the mourners time to assemble, Teferi set the funeral for three days after her death. In throes of grief and dreading the inevitable words from the scoffers "Where is your God?" he fell across the body of his wife that day and urgently called on the name of Jesus. In the presence of her amazed family and many sympathizers, Fitale came back to life. Her relatives appeared more concerned about Jesus having the glory for raising her up than they had about her death.

They waited until Teferi went to work the next morning, and offered a sheep as a sacrifice to the devil, sprinkling its blood all around the house. Realizing what they had done, Teferi became upset when he saw the blood, but he said nothing. Fitale's older brother accosted him, "We are very concerned about our sister. We have offered a sacrifice to the devil and sprinkled blood for her protection. He is ready to kill her again, so you must offer sacrifices regularly to save her life. We expect you to refund the thirty birr we paid for the sheep, and be sure that you make the offerings often."

Teferi fought to control his anger. "I certainly will not pay you for the sheep. In fact, I should take you to court for offering this abominable sacrifice on my premises without my permission. For the Lord's sake I must forgive you, but you can say good-bye to your thirty birr."

Fitale's family, with elders of the town, took Teferi to the village court; the judge said Teferi must refund the money. He appealed to the provincial court, and that judge reversed the decision, fined all concerned, and gave the brother a short jail sentence for trespassing. The family and the village elders who backed them came to Teferi with humble apologies and said, "Truly your Jesus is a wonderful savior. Our idols are sheer vanity. Please forgive us our evil deeds."

Teferi's ordeal opened the door for the church. After fourteen years, Worku returned to Hamusi and proclaimed the gospel in that area with great freedom and good results.

The clever enemy of the church has many weapons to hinder and destroy revival. One of his most frequently used (and often successful) strategies is using the lukewarm to play one believer or leader against another. This snare brought a crisis in the Addis church; however, God's mercy quickly bridged the gap.

Tekle and Erkenesh felt led to return to Negele Borana especially to share the message of Jesus Name baptism and the Oneness of God with those who had received the Holy Ghost on their first visit. On arrival they rented a house for services and a residence for them and their four-month-old daughter, Mehret.

Results came quickly; Five leaders of the Lutheran Church were baptized in the name of Jesus. Then the battle began. Enemies of the truth gave a renegade two hundred birr to kill Tekle and Erkenesh. A teacher named Leta and his wife, Alemitu, heard of the plot and warned them that the man lay in wait for them every night after the people left the meetings. Neither the death threat nor oppressive demonic attacks stopped hungry hearts from obeying the Word. Needing all the help she could find in several dangerous situations, Erkenesh cried out "O Wendells' God, rescue me!" Her and the Wendells' God took care of the need.

Leaders from two groups who were losing members brought Tekle to the police, charging that he preached without a permit, a serious offense. He produced the letter from the emperor, and the police dismissed him and the embarrassed church leaders. After two more weeks of mixed blessings and harassment, an urgent message came from Brother Wendell that Tekle must return to Addis at once. The people who had sold his books did not hand in the money as planned, and the man who signed his note for the printing of the book had been arrested. He had to have two thousand birr immediately.

Before he could go to face that crisis, Tekle had two other problems to solve—who to leave in charge of the work, and how to get money for the trip. The Lord impressed him to turn the new church over to Dejene, a choice that passing years proved wise. He is still a faithful preacher of the gospel in eastern Ethiopia and is a presbyter for the twenty-seven churches he established. Alemitu brought a generous offering, and that paid the bus fare to Addis.

On arrival, Tekle learned with thankfulness that Sophia had paid the outstanding debt and solved his problem.

Unseen Hands

Erkenesh did not allow having a child to hinder her work for the Lord. Many people referred to her and her husband as "the parents who carry their child around in a basket." Erkenesh had fasted more than she should have before Mehret's birth, and frequently they could not find suitable milk for her. Their undernourished five-month-old baby became desperately ill just after they came to Addis. They took the dying child to Brother Wendell, and when he laid his hands on her in the name of Jesus, she received a healing touch from God.

After a discussion with his three deacons, Amare, Teshone and Solomon, Brother Wendell asked Tekle to leave the sixteen churches he supervised and become pastor of the headquarters church in Addis.

"It would certainly suit our flesh to have a nice house and good food and comfort, and not have to travel up and down the country, carrying our baby into all kinds of circumstances," Tekle answered. "If you think it is the will of God, I will do it."

Although he was determined to obey his leader, Tekle was haunted by the thought of those around the country who were ready to be won to the truth; he continually yearned to go find them. He could only put the matter into the hands of the Lord. Brother Wendell came early the next morning and said, "No, Tekle, this is not God's will. Pack your things; I'll take you back to Awasa."

In the midst of unusual revival blessings, Satan craftily slipped a false prophet into the church. Twenty-eight-year-old Temare came with deceptive meekness late in 1970. He gained credibility with a few accurate prophecies, though many things he said could not be understood. He used the people's desire for spirituality and their

Opposition from Within and Without

reverence for the church to maneuver himself into a position of power. If anyone failed to honor his predictions, he foretold of vindictive retributions that happened. He brought the believers into a bondage of fear and deceived everyone, including Tekle.

Brother Wendell noticed that he always found Temare and two cronies sitting in Tekle's tiny apartment at the back of the church. They did not miss a meal or a conversation.

"What do you fellows do for a living?" he asked.

"Oh, we give ourselves to prayer and testimony for the church," Temare answered glibly.

Considering their youth and obvious indolence, the missionary answered sternly, "Stop being a burden to Brother Tekle and his wife. The Bible says that if any would not work, neither should he eat. Go out and get a job and earn your bread honestly."

Temare turned against Brother Wendell from that day and plotted revenge. He soon manipulated Tekle with cunning wiles and threats to write a letter to Brother Wendell, dictated by him. Even after Tekle realized that he had made a mistake and humbly asked forgiveness for the letter, Temare continued to impose his prophet role on the church, for many believed in him.

In May 1971, the United Pentecostal Church sent helpers to the Wendells—John and Jerri Harris and their children, David, Robert, Jonathan, and Jodie, aged from eight to three years. Attending language school to learn the Amharic language was their priority, but Brother Harris's first sermon in Addis is well remembered. He spoke on the ministry of angels (Psalm 34:7). The church would soon have an urgent need for angelic protection.

Soon after his arrival, Brother Harris experienced the pleasure of down-to-earth missionary endeavor. He met the "African bug" (dysentery) on his first trip to Kambata. Only Tekle's earnest prayer through the night helped him to survive.

He stayed in a smoke-filled house at Fiche that did not have a chimney; he wept while preaching for two hours and suffered from a lack of water; he slept on a flea-infested skin; and his slumber was disturbed by the cold nose of a cow next to him in the sleeping order.

Brother Wendell showed Brother Harris the site at Metahara, 150 kilometers north of Addis, that had been granted to the church for a Bible school by the minister of education, who was Sophia's husband. Brother Freeman also saw the land. When the missionaries dug a well for water, the district governor heard that the Pentecostals planned to build in his district; he had the grant cancelled. Brother Wendell could not convince him or any government officials whom he petitioned that he was not a part of the hated, fanatical group known as Pentecostal.

During this confusion, Erkenesh's second child arrived on October 8, 1971. Brother Wendell named the baby Mousse, which means Moses.

For several months the Lord dealt with Erkenesh about things to come. As the Lord showed her what would happen step by step, she wrote it all in a school notebook—the revolution, the overthrow of the emperor, the fate of many politicians, the suffering, the new rulers of the country, and the sweeping changes that would come.

While Tekle ministered in Addis during January 1972, officers arrested Erkenesh as she stood in the pulpit

Opposition from Within and Without

speaking at the beginning of the service. The little notebook containing those dangerous predictions that could spell death for all of them lay on a bench several feet away. At the officer's gruff "Come with me," she held her baby close. She was almost overcome by fright and shock when he pointed to the bench and ordered, "Bring that book with you." Trembling, she picked up the Bible. "No!" he barked. "Bring the notebook with you."

She had thought she was afraid before; now it seemed her violently throbbing heart would leap out of her throat. The officers took all of the believers present to the police station.

As Erkenesh sat across the desk from the officer at the police station, an agony of fear gripped her. She could neither think nor pray as the man twirled the notebook in his hands while he asked her questions. She could barely whisper the expected answers. Suddenly she felt the delicate touch of an unseen presence. She could not see the angel, but he gently stilled the trembling of her body. The fretful baby, terrified in the strange atmosphere, relaxed against his mother.

The officer telephoned the colonel at the headquarter's office, and Erkenesh heard both sides of the conversation.

"Who do you have?" the booming voice on the telephone asked.

"I brought a woman and her baby."

"What did she have?"

"She has a notebook."

She heard his oath as the colonel swore. "Tell her to go home and take her baby and her book with her. We haven't sunk to hounding women with their babies yet."

Erkenesh tore the notebook into little pieces and burned it when she got home. She already knew the contents by heart.

Temare set the stage for the saddest of all internal problems; yet at the end of the story, all concerned could rejoice and testify that Romans 8:28 is true. God makes all things work together for good!

Deep hatred of Brother Wendell moved Temare to make wild predictions against him. He did it slyly behind Tekle's back, because after the letter episode Tekle rebuked him if he said anything against their leader. He had ample opportunity to sow the seeds of bitterness while Tekle traveled to the sixteen churches under his supervision.

The problem came to a head during one of Tekle's trips. Still weak from the difficult birth of Mousse, Erkenesh remained in Awasa in a rented house. Some of Brother Wendell's advisors visited the church and heard Temare vilify Brother Wendell. Motivated by longstanding envy of Tekle, they reported that Tekle was using Temare to fight against the missionaries. They also accused Tekle of teaching many false doctrines, including the "fire fallacy" that tongues of fire is always seen on those filled with the Spirit as on the Day of Pentecost in the upper room.

Kenneth Wendell was suffering from a progressive disease that left his nerves raw, but he felt that he should go to Awasa and investigate the matter. Without authority from Tekle, Temare insisted that the church people miss school and work in order to "fast and pray" at the church on the day that Brother Wendell came.

Opposition from Within and Without

Brother Wendell confronted Temare, "Admit that you prophesy by the power of Satan!"

Temare shouted, "No! I speak by the Spirit of God."

The unannounced session began with a fiery start. After some time, Brother Wendell sent for Erkenesh, and although barely able to walk, she started to the church. Brother Wendell met her a block away to tell her what he wanted her to do. "You must testify to the church that Temare's prophesies are satanic."

In her heart, Erkenesh had doubts of Temare, but fear gripped her. "Brother Wendell, I fear God; I do not know if the man is from Satan or from God. I am afraid to condemn, lest I condemn the Holy Spirit." (Erkenesh had not been able to attend services and really did not know what had been said.) Brother Wendell thought by this that she and Tekle had become his enemies, and he angrily turned back to the church. Erkenesh went home deeply troubled.

Tekle arrived back from Kambata at 6:00 p.m., extremely weary from a long, hard trip. He knew nothing of the whole affair. According to his usual custom he went to the church and bowed his face to the floor in prayer. Brother Wendell had gone to the hotel; one of his advisors hurried to get him. He found Tekle still in prayer and hastily took him by the arm to lift him up so that they could talk. Temare had manipulated the congregation to such a pitch that they wrongly thought Brother Wendell planned to do Tekle bodily harm. They began to pray so loudly that conversation became impossible.

"Do you want to work with me or not?" Brother Wendell yelled so he could be heard over the crescendo of noise.

Completely puzzled, Tekle looked at his saints, then at the missionary. "Is something wrong? Brother Wendell, could you please tell me what is going on?"

Troubled by the whole situation, Brother Wendell left without another word. Tekle felt disturbed when a lady prophesied against Brother Wendell. Tekle dismissed the congregation and went home utterly exhausted. When Tekle and Erkenesh prayed, soon after leaving the church, the Lord told them not to say one word against Brother Wendell or oppose him in any way.

Very early the next morning, Brother Wendell knocked at Tekle and Erkenesh's door. "Tekle, are you there? I want to talk to you," he called.

Groggy from his work and the privations that he had endured, Tekle was disoriented. As he fumbled to find his clothes, anxiety choked him so that he could not find his voice. Brother Wendell called twice more, but by the time Tekle dressed enough to be presentable and opened the door, the missionary was gone.

Back at the hotel, Brother Wendell's aides took advantage of the situation to harp on Tekle's so-called false teaching. "We will never get recognition and respect from this government if they hear about these things being taught in our churches. Something must be done."

Convinced that Tekle had wholly turned against him, Brother Wendell went to the commander of police that morning, November 25, 1971, and stated that the United Pentecostal Church did not endorse or promote the fanaticism that Tekle allowed in the church there.

The commander could care less about differences between the missionary and Tekle, but he saw this as a long-looked-for chance to move against Tekle and the church.

He said, "Write it down for me; I cannot accept verbal accusations."

In his effort to establish the church in the right way, Kenneth Wendell wrote the report, and on his way out of town, gave it to the commander. The police arrested Tekle, Temare, Hailu Fentaw, and Ashenafi, an evangelist, put them in prison, and closed the church, all in the same day.

The police commander telephoned the missionary the next day to come and declare his case against the men. In shock, Brother Wendell explained that he had not meant for any action to be taken against them. He had written the report to make the stand of the church clear in such matters. Not only would he not come and testify against the men, but he begged for their immediate release. When he said, "Let them go," the commander laughed at him and hung up.

The men endured extreme misery in jail. In her weakened condition after a difficult childbirth, Erkenesh could not bring them food or minister to their needs. The court prosecutor brought the case against the men on the day of their trial, based on Brother Wendell's report. He read their names and said, "These men are guilty of teaching doctrines contrary to the Pentecostal church."

This threw the court into confusion. The whole legal system had been geared against the Pentecostals according to the emperor's decree. As Pentecostals, they would be judged guilty, whatever the charges. But the words "doctrines contrary to the Pentecostals" put them on the other side of the fence. Since the judges did not know what else to do, they sent them back to jail and postponed the case.

The believers opened the church again in spite of threats and in spite of the officers who came into the church frequently, yelling, "Stop this service."

After the fiasco of a trial, Tekle took full responsibility for the charges, asked the police to release the three other men charged with him, and appealed to be tried by the high court. The three men were released on bail.

The high court saw that the charges against Tekle contradicted the circular against Pentecostals and declared him innocent. The general sent an order changing the charge to preaching without a license. Tekle produced the license given him by the emperor and the state church. The authorities delayed his release as long as possible but had to let him go on February 10, 1972.

Thanks to Brother Wendell's charge, Tekle escaped the persecution of that time, for the charge officially labeled him as a non-Pentecostal. In her ordeal with the notebook, Erkenesh found a freedom from fear that remained with her throughout the trials ahead. They rejoiced in Jesus, who makes all things work together for good.

John Harris, Tekle and E. L. Freeman.

13

In the Furnace

Tekle opened the church again after his release. Two weeks later, an extraordinary deluge of the Holy Ghost fell on the congregation with visible tongues of fire, as in Acts 2. A move of God's Spirit as powerful as electricity swept from the church; people riding bicycles in front of the building leaped from their vehicles and ran away. Never had such a variety of miracles occurred in one day.

Tekle did not teach that this must happen when the Holy Ghost comes; he only said, "The Lord sent fire once and He can do it again." The three deacons took this as evidence for their contention that Tekle taught false doctrines, despite that believers in Addis experienced the same manifestation that Sunday.

For some time the police had frequently interrupted the church services, taking believers to the police station, beating them, and mistreating them. Neighbors advised the believers to stop having church. When the believers refused, the neighbors offered, "Then give us your children, for you will surely be killed."

"No," the saints replied. "We will take our children with us; if we die, we will die together."

After the plot to imprison Tekle failed, the police and officials of the state church concocted another scheme, hoping to kill Tekle this time. Not knowing that Tekle had gone to Addis for a few days, they gathered a mob of about six thousand people and stirred them up to attack the Pentecostals.

They surrounded the rented church building on Wednesday night, March 29, 1972, armed with sticks, iron stakes, and fence posts with large nails protruding that they had jerked up from around the property. They brought kerosene to burn Bibles, benches, and whatever else they found.

Entranced in prayer and worship, the congregation did not know the mob had come against them.

"You!" Erkenesh opened her eyes in surprise when she heard the loud voice of a policeman who stood before her.

"If you will stop this loud praying and screaming 'Hallelujah' and break up this so-called church, we will not harm you. But," he spoke sternly, "if you persist you will be killed."

Erkenesh calmly looked into his eyes and answered in a clear voice, "We will never stop praising Jesus. He has done wonderful things for us." When Erkenesh would not listen, the policeman went to the preacher. Taking his hand, he pulled him from the church and helped him to escape before giving the signal for attack.

Fury exploded around the congregation. Erkenesh and the baby in her arms were clubbed. The mob beat, strangled and jerked the believers until all of them, about seventy-five people, lay unconscious. While the attackers waited for trucks to take the people to the health center, they vented their anger on everything that they could find. They broke or burned benches, tracts, Bibles, and Tekle's household effects and splintered the doors and windows of the building.

Neighbors carried Ernenesh to their home, and when she regained consciousness the next morning, she found Mousse in great pain from his injuries. Hailu's wife had shielded Mehret in her arms and had suffered only one blow on the side of her head. Mehret was not harmed.

When the trucks arrived, the attackers pitched the injured people into them, using as much care as would be given to cord wood. Touched by the Spirit of God, on arriving at the clinic the wounded climbed from the trucks and joyfully returned home. Miraculously, all the other children escaped injury.

Tekle had planned to return home on March 22, and he told his hostess, Salome, good-bye. On the way to catch the bus, an invisible band fastened around his feet and held him.

"Salome, do you see chains or something holding me?" he asked. Neither of them could see anything. When he decided to visit other believers and wait until the next day to go home, his feet moved freely. For five days the strange pattern repeated in the same way. If he thought to go witness or encourage someone, his feet would move, but when he said, "I am going home," the power holding his feet returned.

On the third day Tekle asked an evangelist to fast and pray with him about the mystery of his feet taking odd spells of refusing to move. On the evening of the sixth

Unseen Hands

day, March 29, a telephone call came warning him not to come to Awasa; men waited to kill him.

Erkenesh's six-month-old son suffered for a week and died, which brought another dilemma. The town would not allow the Pentecostals a place to bury their dead. If she let Tekle know the baby was dead, he would come, giving the armed police the chance they sought to kill him. The child's funeral would possibly trigger another attack, even if a burial place could be found. She cried to the Lord, "Please put life in my baby and make a way for me to take him to Addis." The child started breathing again. While the police guarded the front door, Erkenesh slipped out the back door. She left Awasa at 5:00 a.m. and changed buses six times (almost every town). The buses frequently broke down. The road to Addis seemed unending, and the heart of a mother breathed silent prayers all the way for her suffering child. She reached Addis at 5:00 p.m.

Everyone at Salome's house gathered around the infant on the evening she reached Addis, praying for the baby's recovery. While they prayed, God gave Tekle three visions in quick succession. In the first he toured hospitals and saw children of all races cruelly mangled, blinded, and crippled. The Lord spoke, "Do not pray for your son; pray for these children who have no one to care for them."

In the second vision he saw a towering mountain, rough and rugged, with people wandering aimlessly up and down and around and around. "They need someone to show them the right road to travel," he heard.

Then the heavens opened, and he saw a city made of round, golden stones as bright as the sun. A colossal, shining palace of beauty beyond description stood in the center of the city, surrounded by exquisite trees that never have been seen on earth. While he gazed on this scene, the baby died. The Lord said, "This is your son's new home. Do not grieve for him."

Salome's family began to weep and mourn for the baby as they arrived.

"We are not to weep," Tekle told them. "God has taken our child to His abode." Instead of grief, a sweet spirit of praise swept over Erkenesh. To the amazement of the saints, she rejoiced and worshiped from a heart strangely filled with joy.

With much effort, Lakew, Salome's Catholic son-in-law, obtained permission for the baby to be buried in his own plot in the Catholic cemetery. Tekle took charge of the funeral service and spoke with an anointing that changed lives—Lakew's first of all.

Disaster befell the agitators of the attack on the church in Awasa. The colonel and the Coptic priest went home to empty houses—everything they possessed had vanished. They were told that thieves had stripped their houses, but no clues as to whom were ever found. The daughter of another agitator was struck by lightning and killed instantly. Two more were murdered mysteriously, and three committed suicide. One went to jail for manslaughter, and another cut off his own hand while butchering an ox. With blood spurting from his arm, he ran through the town screaming, "You were the hand that beat the innocent Pentecostals." A hurricane wind demolished a portion of the town, and many, confessing it to be divine judgment, cried to the Lord for forgiveness.

One of the ringleaders went to the ruined church and lifted his hands, saying, "Thank you, Holy Trinity, that

Unseen Hands

we could destroy this work." Within a short time, he had a stroke that left him paralyzed and mindless. He was treated in hospitals for two years without improvement. A witch doctor bathed him in blood regularly and performed many other rituals for a year, without results. His family took him home to die. Later, one of the beaten men, Hailu, prayed for him, and his mind partially returned. Today his wife is a born again member of the new Apostolic church that Hailu built and is pastor in Awasa. He walks with a cane as a reminder of God's mercy.

According to ancient Ethiopian tradition, every acquaintance of a deceased person is expected to attend the funeral, and someone not buried in a church cemetery is considered lost and without God. Since Apostolics are denied the right to church cemeteries, their faith must supersede tradition.

Erkenesh's older sister Bizunesh knew her one-year-old infant could not live. She and her husband traveled to a remote area where graves could be dug. One week after the death of Moses, five strangers helped them bury their little one. Later another believer named Molash, took her sick baby to Addis and returned to Awasa to care for the rest of her family. Tekle and Erkenesh helped Mamo, the father, find a place to bury the child. When the baby died, Molash was unable to attend the funeral.

On the many trips Brother Freeman made to Ethiopia, on my first visit in 1971, and during the latter trips of others—the Doyle Spearses, C. G. Weeks, and T. L. Craft—all of us saw the evident tokens of cataclysmic upheaval ahead. The first week of April, Brother Wendell called Brother Freeman, regional field supervisor for Africa. "Come and help us," he requested. "The church

In the Furnace

has been banned. A time has been set for the last service, and we Americans have to leave."

Brother Freeman went and helped them in every way possible. He talked to many officials, made a vain attempt to see the emperor, and tried to encourage the missionaries. Nothing could be done to extend the existence of the United Pentecostal Church in Ethiopia. On Tekle's suggestion, they changed the name to the Apostolic Church of Ethiopia, hoping that elimination of the word *Pentecostal* would help the work to survive.

The only avenue of service possible would be under the auspices of a school. Brother Wendell bought land in the name of his deacon Amare, and the believers quickly built the modest Apostle Peter's School to serve as both an elementary school and a limited outreach. They secreted a small baptistery under the floor.

The time came for the last service. Both missionaries refused to preach. "It is as if we are preaching our own funeral," they said.

God gave Brother Freeman a message of faith. Among other things he said, "The early church operated illegally most of the time, but they reached the known world in a short time. You may be temporarily deprived of regular services as you have known in the past, but no decree can annul the power of the Holy Ghost that you have in your heart.

"Use the Holy Ghost's power! You cannot go in pairs, but you can win souls one by one. Find a hungry heart; love and teach and pray until that one is filled with God's Spirit. Send him to the workers to be baptized in the name of Jesus and then find another hungry heart. Remember, the name of Jesus cannot fail. We will ask the churches around the world to pray for you, and I will return when God makes it possible."

Brother Freeman left soon after that service. The two oldest Wendell children had gone back to America the year before, and Sister Wendell, Jeanie, and Chet left in April. Tekle and Erkenesh grieved over the departure of the missionaries and went to Addis to be with them in their last days in the land. They asked forgiveness again for the misunderstandings of the past and enjoyed restored fellowship. The three deacons made another attempt to drive a wedge between them, but this time they did not succeed.

Brother Wendell left Ethiopia in June 1972 after making his deacons, Amare, Teshome, and Solomon, board members and designating Ashenafi Andargei and Negussie Haile as evangelists. The John Harris family transferred to Kenya in the same month to found the United Pentecostal Church there.

The atrocious attack on the church at Awasa had probably been triggered by Tekle's baptizing Hailu Fantaw, a Coptic church official, in Jesus' name. Fear that more church leaders would follow his example stirred the persecutors to make new plans to eliminate Tekle and his followers. They widely distributed a circular asking anyone who found Tekle to kill him at once, and they threatened to burn the homes of believers while they slept at night.

On November 23, 1973, Tekle and Erkenesh went to Addis to appeal to the emperor. The emperor often granted favors, money, and land to those who managed to get to him through the barricade of guards. No common person could come in the palace to see him, but if

In the Furnace

a woman approached him on the street he would often listen to her request. (He feared a man might try to kill him.)

While Tekle prayed, Erkenesh waited for Emperor Haile Selassie where she knew he would pass. Soldiers surrounded her with guns, but the emperor motioned her to the side of the car. He listened while she told him about her son's being killed by a police-ordered attack and about the circular letter. He took her to the palace, treated her kindly, and telephoned the chief of police to investigate the letter of instruction to kill on sight.

Tekle and Erkenesh returned to Awasa with a letter ordering the circular to be withdrawn. They then faced the serious problem of housing. The building they rented before had been nearly demolished, and no one in the city would rent a building of any kind to them or to their members. This effectively scattered the church, an episode repeated in all the places where they had ministered. Many saints languished in prison, and fear paralyzed the rest.

Word spread that Erkenesh had spoken to the emperor, and that Tekle had received compensation for the death of his son. The owners of the damaged building came demanding their share. Nothing remained for Tekle and Erkenesh to do but to return to Addis. They had no idea of the desert experience ahead.

Friends who had been gracious in the past now refused to entertain the fugitives for fear of reprisals. They went to a hotel, and three days later their money ran out. They had no idea what to do or where to go, but as Tekle walked out on the verandah of the hotel he saw a young man, Kaleab, running toward him. "The Lord told me to give you this," he announced, handing him thirty birr.

Without furnishings and without knowing where the rent would come from, they felt led to rent a small house. A few days later a young man from Awasa found them. He had moved to Harar and had looked for them from Awasa to Addis. He held out 195 birr, explaining, "This is tithe money that I saved for you."

After a short time of peace, a policeman who had transferred from Awasa spotted Tekle. He hurried to Coptic church leaders and told them, "The man who did much harm to the church in Awasa is here. He is not fit to live." They decided to burn the house down over them, but the landlord heard of it and evicted Tekle without notice saving them from death by fire.

One of Erkenesh's brothers who lived in Nakanisa, a suburb of Addis, allowed them to stay in a small, miserable outside building at his home. Even though he highly disapproved of their work for the Lord, he came every day and wept over their sad condition, wanting to find work for them. This could not be God's will, and they knew it. Under insistent pressure and often without food, Tekle became extremely ill. The brother took his family with him on an overseas scholarship and let them move into a more comfortable room in his house. With much prayer Tekle recovered.

Tekle and Erkenesh met two old friends from their former fellowship. They said, "The Lord has told us to bring our tithes to you. We want nothing to do with your baptism, but we will obey the Lord."

After they moved to another house in the southern part of the city, Erkenesh had their third child, a boy, on July 30, 1973. She named him Eyosias, after King

In the Furnace

Josiah, who pulled down the idols in Jerusalem. She deeply desired that the Lord would remove all idols and every hindrance to the free spread of the gospel in Ethiopia.

Strangely enough, that year marked the beginning of the end of the Coptic church's stranglehold on the land of Ethiopia. Communists took over the government and abolished longstanding, foolish, unbiblical traditions and idolatrous festive occasions, which had been commonly practiced for thousands of years.

The money the two young friends brought every month kept Tekle and Erkenesh alive for nearly a year, though Erkenesh felt troubled by the situation. Finally she had to speak. "Above everything we want your souls to be saved. I feel so badly about accepting your tithes for nothing. Please do not be offended, but do not bring the money again unless you are ready to accept the truth." That ended the income. Eleven years later one of the young men, Kaleab, and some of his family accepted the truth and were baptized in the name of Jesus.

Worry overwhelmed Tekle as Erkenesh lay with her new baby, and they had not one bit of food in the house. He went to a store nearby and asked if they would give him thirty birr worth of food on credit to be paid in a month. As he approached his home, carrying the bag of groceries, he felt a rebuke from the Lord: Why have you made this debt, and how will you pay it? Then he realized that he should have trusted the Lord. Taking the foodstuff back would be too embarrassing; having chosen his road, he had to walk it.

A few gifts of food or occasionally an item of clothing came to their house in the next three months, but no money. Tekle's debt haunted him; he refused to walk by the shop that gave him credit.

With nine mouths to feed, from early morning until the afternoon, Erkenesh desperately called on the Lord to provide. Her sister Ayalesh, her husband, Bekele, and their daughter came to visit, bringing a gift of food. As she served them, Erkenesh told them, "You are God's ravens, an answer to my prayer." They had planned to shop for new clothes, but instead they went to town and made generous purchases to meet the needs of the household.

One of the families that had rejected Tekle and Erkenesh when they first came to Addis were led astray by a family member who proclaimed, "The Apostolic church is dead. Return to the Orthodox church." Trouble came; the mother of the family lost her mind. They contacted Tekle with an urgent plea, "Please come and pray." God restored her after three weeks and gave a true prophecy through her: "These things have come on us because we have forsaken the true church." They became Apostolics again and brought Tekle a gift of three hundred birr.

Tekle made the Lord a solemn promise never again to waver in trusting Him, and he paid his overdue debt with an apology.

This proved to be the time for change. Scattered believers whom Tekle had brought to the Lord or baptized came to stand with him again, and those who had feared to allow him and Erkenesh in their homes came repenting. Tekle only baptized seven souls in two years in Addis, but now from their dark corners of discouragement God gathered a small flock that needed a shepherd.

In the Furnace

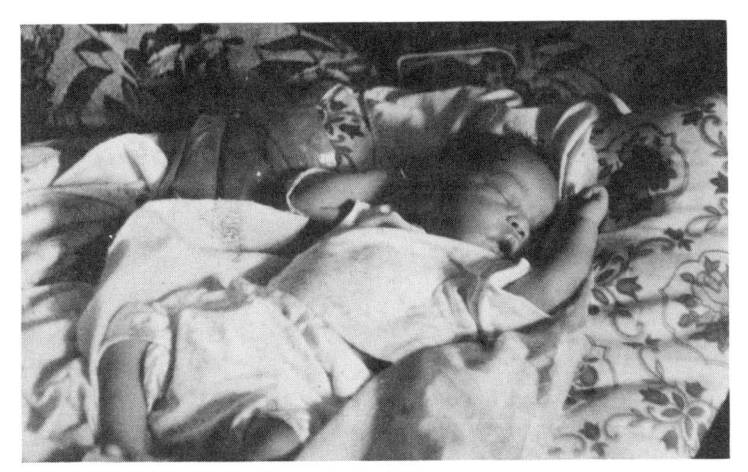

Baby Moses, killed at six months.

Mountain top seminar.

Unseen Hands

Baptizing.

Preaching in the countryside.

14

Molding a Church

On a brief visit early in 1973, Brother Freeman found the ban effective. Of sixteen churches, only those in remote places dared to hold services. No one knew how many of the approximately twelve hundred believers still held the faith. The lepers disappeared soon after the ban, and persecution whittled the Addis church considerably. A few people worked with the board members in secret, uneasily. The nickname "Pentes" for the Pentecostals had surfaced earlier as an expression of increased contempt, and Brother Freeman thanked God for the church's name change.

The supervisor found no indications that Amare would become a dedicated leader. His main concern seemed to be income from the school. Tekle still wandered on the "backside of the desert."

Just after Bro. Freeman's visit, Tekle had a vision of a magnificent, towering, glossy-green tree spreading an abundance of fruitful branches as far as he could see. "This is My church; I am the tree," the Lord said. Tekle remembered His words in John 15:5: "I am the vine, ye are the branches."

The church cannot exist as a small, isolated branch; it must be one with the tree...the vine, Tekle thought. The church has authority to bind and to loose in the name of Jesus, and it will be greatly blessed by unity. Each branch must supply and share its God-given responsibility as illustrated by I Corinthians 3:6: "I have planted, Apollos watered; but God gave the increase." I will pastor the flock the Lord has given me and work untiringly for the body to become one. We will follow the teaching of the Bible and the United Pentecostal Church as Brother Wendell taught us.

Brother Harris had been appointed superintendent of Ethiopia just after he went to Kenya in 1972. Brother Freeman went with him to visit the work as often as possible. Early in 1974 they found services in progress again, since the emperor had to give his undivided attention to maintaining his power. Political turmoil gripped the land in vicelike tentacles; the country bristled with intrigue, tension, and unexplained murders. Both missionaries felt disturbed over the lack of progress in the work under Amare.

Erkenesh had her fourth child on April 16, 1975. His parents named him Abraham, believing that God would pour out the blessing of Abraham on them and the church. This came to pass before the year ended.

Tekle let it be known that he wanted to bridge the gap between the two works led by him and Amare, and three ladies from Amare's group felt God's leading to be mediators. When they approached their pastor, he answered haughtily, "I cannot work with Tekle; he teaches false doctrines."

Sisters Kelelmua, Yeub-dar, and Workei asked Tekle about this. He responded, "Please tell Amare that I strictly preach United Pentecostal Church doctrines."

With that message, the Lord anointed the ladies to point out that God desires unity among his children and that Satan is the author of division. The board members finally agreed, without enthusiasm, to a reconciliation meeting to be held at the home of Mother Salome.

The Lord gave Tekle Micah 6:7-8, making him understand that whatever the brothers said his answers must be humble. The meeting began with a flat accusation: "Tekle, you are a heretic; you teach falsely."

"If I have taught wrongly, please forgive me," Tekle answered gently. "I promise to adhere exactly to the teaching of the United Pentecostal Church from now on."

Tekle did not know what the board members planned to do. The church had to have a strong leader, and they wanted to eliminate Tekle as a possible leader. They went down the line, making accusations point by point, and Tekle answered each one with the same words. He neither raised his voice nor became impatient with their insistent needling. His humility impressed believers from both groups and they all agreed that the two works should become one. However, Amare rented a room in Workie's house for meetings without recognizing Tekle as a fellow minister.

Brother Harris came to help elect a leader for the church, and he appointed a committee to supervise the election: Brothers Teshome and Bekele and himself. The voting began with a secret ballot. When Brother Harris saw extra votes from people who had never been members padding the ballot box, he sternly limited voting to the ministry.

Tekle won the election by a large margin. Amare became his assistant; Teshome, the treasurer; and Erkenesh, the secretary. Instead of being in a desert, Tekle now found himself in quicksand. The board members ignored him and held their own secret meetings, making decisions that hampered the work.

They first decided that the leader and his assistant should receive only fifty birr a month out of the tithes. This was no hardship for Amare: he had the income from the school, and only his wife to support. Tekle had his wife, three children, his mother, and two sisters who depended on him. This effectively confined him to Addis, making it impossible for him to visit and encourage the other churches. He could neither make calls on saints living at a distance in the city, nor buy sufficient food; he paid forty birr a month in rent alone.

Danger mounted in Addis when the communists toppled the emperor's regime in September 1974, and a time of unprecedented violence swept the city as factions backed by China and Russia continued a tug of war for control.

Having rendered Tekle helpless, Amare took control of the work with careless disregard of the consequences. The revival stopped, and weak believers fell away. At a time when the church needed strength to minister to the uprooted and devastated, it had only a carnal power struggle. Tekle patiently waited on the Lord while the board members ruled that he could not preach in Addis. Tekle and Erkenesh could only cry to the Lord for help. In May, Brother Harris wrote to Tekle as the official leader say-

Molding a Church

ing that God had impressed him to tell the brothers to start many churches in Addis instead of staying together in one group. Addis could not be reached without evangelism.

When Tekle read the letter to the board members, they scornfully rejected the counsel of Brother Harris. In answer to a query from Brother Harris about their reactions, Tekle had to relay their refusal to do as advised. Brother Harris then asked Tekle to prepare an agenda for a meeting to settle the problem.

In May 1975, Brother Harris and Brother Donald Ikerd (who began a missionary term in Kenya in 1974) came to help untangle the snarl. When they showed Amare the agenda that Brother Harris had asked Tekle to prepare, Amare became angry and the board members walked out of the first service. Brothers Harris and Ikerd both preached that evening in the rented church. On the second day, thirteen preachers who had come from other districts found the door locked and a notice posted by Amare which said that no meetings would be held in that room with foreigners. Boycotted by the board members, the preachers moved the gathering to Tekle's residence, where both missionaries preached again on unity in the morning service.

The agenda Tekle prepared had three points:

1. The school must be turned over to the church and changed to a Bible school. The preachers should stop teaching children to read; they should develop their ministry in God's Word.

2. The evangelists should not confine their efforts to the Addis church but should start evangelizing.

3. The duties and the authority of the superintendent

should be clearly defined.

The board members came to the afternoon meeting. They demanded that the ministers meeting be postponed, and they promised to bring written charges against Tekle when the meeting resumed the next day.

They returned after an all-night session and made the following statements:

1. Tekle's two tracts, one on the new birth and the other asking if the reader desired salvation, were not scriptural. (They had commended and freely distributed the tracts up to that time.)

2. They could not give the school to the church; they depended on it for a living. They wanted to continue teaching and to witness for the Lord in their spare time.

3. Tekle had defamed them in letters to Brother Harris.

4. They insisted that they did not need Tekle's leadership, saying, "We are grown men and can direct ourselves. We have the Spirit to lead us. We do not want Tekle to come to us except by invitation."

Brother Harris immediately appointed three men to examine the tracts: Hailu Wolde-Tsadik, Bekele Feyye, and Wolde-Giorgis. Answering the third point, he said, "Brother Tekle did not defame you to me. You are our brethren; in good faith, I have handed a gift of $2,400 for the expenses of this meeting to our treasurer, Brother Teshome."

Discussion on the other points became heated with the board members doing most of the talking. At one point, one of them asked for the floor and turned to Brother Harris. "You are not our superintendent," he said, "and you should be silenced!"

Molding a Church

Brother Ikerd rebuked him sharply, with the approval of the other preachers, then gave them a detailed lesson on church organization and proper conduct for ministers.

On the third day of the conference, the three brothers reported on the tracts in question. "They are well written and completely scriptural."

The missionaries' admonitions and pleas for unity did not affect the board members, who continued to pour their verbal animosity on the gathering. Finally, Brother Harris suggested a recess, but before he could ask anyone to dismiss the meeting, a heavy spirit of prayer fell on every sincere person in the room. Simultaneously they called on the name of the Lord. Suddenly, Tekle stood, shaking as a leaf in the wind and spoke in trumpet tones. "I command the demons who are hindering God's work to leave this room at once." A chill settled over the place, and Amare and his four cronies stalked out.

Some time later, after dismissal, Brother Harris asked a question. "Tekle, would you be willing to step down and just pastor your church and let Amare be superintendent?"

"I will be happy to do that, or anything you suggest, if I can only remain in fellowship with the United Pentecostal Church," Tekle answered humbly.

The missionaries went back to the hotel to seek God's will and wisdom. The Lord impressed Brother Ikerd to read I Kings 12:21-24. In that passage God restrained Rehoboam when he wanted to fight to unite Israel and Judah and sent His prophet to say, "This thing is from me." The missionaries went to Tekle at once and told him, "Get together the preachers who are willing to obey the discipline of the church. Now we know what to do."

Brother Ikerd read the passage of Scripture to those in the meeting and explained the leading of the Lord. Thirteen preachers and the two missionaries voted to disfellowship the five rebellious men and wrote official letters stating their decision to each of them according to his position.

Amare kept the school, and creating the next crisis, Teshome refused to return the expense money that Brother Harris had brought or any of the funds in the church account. The preachers who had come from various distances had neither food nor means to return home. The missionaries had given all they could to Teshome and could not give more. Sad countenances faced Tekle.

"We have to trust the Lord, brothers," he comforted. "He knows our need."

At that moment Sophia knocked on the door. "The Lord told me to give you this," she said holding a thousand birr. "You will know where it is needed."

He knew!

The missionaries returned to Kenya after appointing a new board: Tekle, superintendent; Bekele Feyye, treasurer; Hailu Wolde-Tsadik, presbyter; and Erkenesh, secretary and Ladies Auxiliary leader. Although lacking in natural resources, they had oneness of spirit and purpose. The open sewer running under Tekle's house made services unpleasant, and he lost many members who tolerated Amare in order to worship in a nicer room rented from Workei. Tekle's work made slow progress, while the church under Amare expanded rapidly.

Upheaval and violence in the city touched the church. A man with a machine gun burst into Tekle's house during a Sunday morning service. From the confused look on his face, they surmised that he meant to say "Hands up!" but he said, "Get out!" Everyone trooped outside and stood before him. He shook his head as if dazed, and lowering the gun, he turned away saying, "I'll come back another day and take action against you." The next day, the authorities transferred him to a different job, and he fell dead at this new post.

A few weeks later, his well-armed partner came to Erkenesh and threatened, "My late friend told you to stop holding church, and you disregarded his warning. If I find you gathered together again, praying in this house, I will kill all of you." An enemy of his shot and killed him that evening.

In those perilous days, men often misused their authority to settle old grudges, pretending they were wiping out government opposition. One of those decided to kill all church leaders and especially the "Pentes." The night he waylaid Tekle, something happened to his usually accurate aim. The bullet only fanned Tekle's hair. Found to be antigovernment a few days later, the man and his accomplices suffered the fate that he planned for Tekle, who was safe in the care of Jesus.

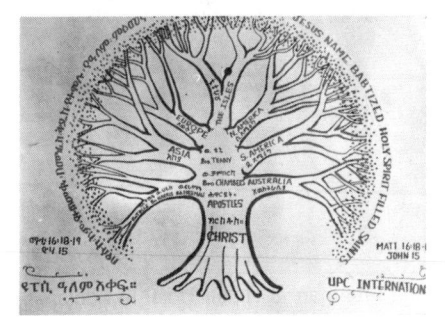

Tekle's vision of the church as a tree.

Unseen Hands

Tekle's family before birth of Joshua.

Tekle and Erkenesh with Nona Freeman at Hilton Hotel in Addis.

15

God Sends Revival

The church that God desired to be one had split with a finality that could not be mended. Tekle's fragment of it appeared as a frail flower about to droop and be lost in oblivion. The change did not come suddenly, with drum rolls or heralding trumpets. It even took Tekle a while to comprehend the scope of God's exciting plan. God called people from every walk of life, and they became soul winners. Farmers, merchants, university architecture and engineering students, common laborers, government employees, high school graduates and woodworkers all felt the touch of the Master and could never be the same again.

By the end of 1975, twenty-four men dedicated themselves to take the gospel wherever God led. No one planned psychologically touching services to persuade them to work for the Lord—God called them. With trust only in Jesus, the provider, and with determined respect and confidence in Tekle, their God-appointed leader, they went without promises of support or security. They did not allow the political chaos of the land or constant threats of prison and death to deter them. No new work opened in 1972, 1973, or 1974, but the close of 1975 saw twenty-four new churches established, with 6,346 new converts baptized in the name of Jesus.

The smelly place of worship no longer hindered Tekle's church in Addis. Ignoring the putrid odor of sewage, the hungry-hearted came to be filled and healed. Rich blessings from the Lord of the Harvest brought a bounty of souls that overflowed the inadequate quarters.

Excitement clouded my eyes as we landed at the Addis Ababa airport in February 1976 for my first visit since 1971. I immediately became conscious of the dramatic changes—some beneficial—that the country had undergone. After a joyous meeting with Erkenesh (Tekle came later), I offered sympathy on the death of her baby in 1972.

"He is happy before God's throne," she smiled, "and he is no longer hungry or cold."

Along with the joys of seeing dear, familiar faces again, we had lengthy, serious discussions about the future of the work. Many churches had been closed and their buildings confiscated for use by the government.

Working in several communist countries, we understood the preciousness of every fragile moment to fulfill our calling. Late that Saturday night my husband turned to me and said, "As foreigners, our presence here may be more of a handicap than a benefit. Give them the very best message that you can in the service tomorrow, dear. You might not come back for a long time."

I prayed throughout the night for "the very best message" ever and felt decidedly dissatisfied with the only thought that the Lord gave me—Ephesians 5:20: "Giving thanks always for all things unto God," and a companion statement in Hebrews 13:15: "By him therefore let us offer the sacrifice of praise to God continually, that is, the fruit of our lips giving thanks to his name." The more I prayed, the more definitely the sermon came, with dozens of verses of Scripture flashing in my mind.

A young man came to get us, and on the way to church, I heard for the first time the story of the old Dutchman whom God used as a signpost to point toward the mighty outpouring of the Holy Ghost destined to come to Ethiopia.

"I am Ayele, Marta's son and Salome's grandson," he explained, "and best of all, I am now a child of God! I received the Holy Ghost six weeks ago, and the old Dutchman's prophecy might come true after all."

People flowed over into three rooms of the house where the church met, and a sweet spirit of worship prevailed from the start. Suddenly, a young girl fell to the floor screaming and pulling her hair, being tormented by evil spirits. Deliverance came in minutes by the power of the name of Jesus. The scene was repeated a few minutes later with an older woman. Then a man led his son forward. I noticed the son's darting eyes of insanity as the two of them stood before my husband and Tekle. After prayer Tekle told the father to loose him. I did not realize that his hands were tightly bound until he removed the *gabe,* a gauzy white stole worn by both sexes against chilly, high-altitude mornings and evenings. The father slowly untied the ropes, explaining how violent the boy had been. Once free, the son merely rubbed his hands together to restore circulation and smiled shyly with normal eyes.

After my husband brought a tremendous sermon on the unlimited power of God, my turn came to preach. Doubts about my topic disappeared as the message flowed with the Spirit. I became convinced more than ever that our approach to serving the Lord is often backwards, and I presented this message to the people. We often wait until we receive healing or protection or the solution to a problem before we praise the Lord. Instead, we need to praise Him *first*—for the sickness, for the danger, and for the problem—offering a sacrifice of praise in the midst of trials.

For many years, I did not realize that the word *for* carried with it such explicit instructions. Understanding that these precious people had gone through life-changing upheavals and could face many more situations fraught with danger and uncertainty, I realized that the Lord had put a special weapon into their hands to help them or anyone else who obeys the biblical admonition to give "thanks always for all things."

Yakob, a policeman, tried every avenue of medical resources, ancient and modern, without relief. Even prayer did not remove the agony from his stomach. Tekle called on the saints to join him in fasting and prayer for Yakob's healing. Shortly afterward Yakob passed a hairy creature the size of a large frog. He kept the parasite pickled in a bottle for a long time and witnessed constantly of the limitless power of Jesus.

Disgusted with his witnessing, his boss transferred him to Aleta-Wondo and loaded him with duties. This did not hinder him. He paid the transportation costs to bring his first converts to Awasa for baptism. He won Zerihune to the Lord and started the church at Aleta-Wondo where Zerihune long served as pastor.

The more souls he brought in, the more angry his boss became and repeatedly ordered him to stop. When he would not, the boss transferred him to a lonely, waterless border post in the desert and withheld his salary for three months. Faithful Yakob would not desert his responsibility, and he starved to death. Since that time eighty thousand souls have found God in the region where he founded the church. From 1974 to 1977 countless people died violently in Ethiopia. Miraculously, frequent attempts on the lives of the church people failed; Yakob was the only fatality during that time.

Bekele Feyye is the genial, sweet-spirited secretary-treasurer of the Apostolic Church of Ethiopia. He has come a long way. When he and Tekle lived in Awasa, he worked for the minister of finance and served as a faithful deacon in the Coptic church. He suffered from demon possession for six years, having seizures that caused him to fall headlong unconscious, foaming at the mouth and screaming, and to remain in that state for hours.

He tried numerous hospitals and "holy water" cures and traveled thousands of kilometers to famous witch doctors. He spent everything that he had trying to find relief. Nothing helped.

One day, his colleague Yakob brought him to church, and one simple prayer in the almighty Name drove eight hundred demons out of him. He found not only deliverance but also salvation. His wife and son had endured such afflictions that Tekle called it a "destroyed" household. They received the same blessed benefits as Bekele and have been tireless soul winners ever since.

Unseen Hands

Mamo Asres heard of Tekle, and while he had no interest for himself, he told a friend who had a paralyzed son, "They say this man prays for the sick and they are instantly healed. He could probably cure your son."

"Would you ask him to come pray for my son?" his friend asked. "Of course, I do not plan to be converted, but I would even be baptized to get my son healed. I could return to my own church afterwards."

Tekle and Erkenesh refused to give Mamo an answer until they prayed about the matter. When Tekle came to Mamo, he said, "No, we cannot go."

Erkenesh added, "We felt troubled by the leading of the Lord not to pray for the boy, but He told us: Go ahead; if you want to go alone, you may. I will not go with you. This man only wants healing for his son, he does not want Me."

Mamo marvelled at Jesus, who knows the hearts of all men, and asked, "What can I do to be saved?"

Tekle happily answered that question in great detail, using numerous verses of Scripture. Then Mamo surprised him by saying, "I will not go home until you baptize me in that beautiful name."

Coming from the river, Mamo insisted that Tekle and Erkenesh go home with him to meet his family. They saw his four-year-old daughter who could not walk and prayed for her before they left. Nothing happened when they asked the Lord to heal her, and in the Ethiopian manner Mamo walked to the edge of his premises with his guests. When he returned to the house, he found the child walking!

Bisrat Desta, currently the Ladies Auxiliary leader in Awasa, became seriously ill at the time her baby should have been born. Doctors discovered that the baby had died and told the family to take the mother home to die; she could not live. Tekle encouraged them to believe God, who can raise the dead. "Station someone at the door to tell everyone that she lives, and do not weep, even if she appears to be dead. We will pray."

After a lengthy time of prayer, the dead baby arrived, and the mother appeared lifeless, with no vital signs. "Now we will really pray," Tekle declared. Several hours later, her body became warm. Soon Bisrat opened her eyes and asked, "Where have I been?" She is a living, healthy testimony of God's power and the wife of the present pastor at Awasa.

The Lord did these mighty works at Awasa at a time of church closings in other areas. The church there received a large grant of land. With a small amount of help from the Foreign Missions Division, in 1977 they completed a church building that is a testimony to the King of kings.

When the Harris family went on furlough in 1976, Brother and Sister Don Ikerd came to Awasa for a conference and visited some of the country works. At that time Russian-inspired communists, with the help of Cubans, were subjecting the people by artillery. To bless the Apostolic churches, the Ikerds faced danger, inconveniences, and lack of suitable lodging and food; however, they joyfully endured it all.

When the time came for the return to Addis, the Ikerds were pushed three times from the bus they were trying to board by a force they could not understand. They waited long in the midst of utter confusion, before Tekle told them to get in a certain car. Down the road they found that the bus they first tried to board had hit another bus head-on, killing all passengers.

They passed numerous police checkpoints where everyone stopped except their driver. He kept going, and no one tried to stop him. They tried to communicate with him, but he ignored them. Sharon Ikerd looked over his shoulder and saw a machine gun in his lap. In Addis, she looked up and said, "Oh, there's our hotel." The driver pulled to the curb immediately, and as soon as they got out of the car, he zoomed away without a word. They remember with joy their "gun-toting angel."

Just after Tekle came home from the UPCI World Conference in Jerusalem, his new daughter arrived on January 1, 1977. They named her Jerusalem in memory of his trip and with the deeper significance of faith that the dream of a headquarters church building in Addis would become reality—a Jerusalem for the church of Ethiopia.

After all other remedies failed, long-blind Dengore came to the Apostolic church for prayer. Seventy demons came out of her, and she received her sight. The leader of them told his name: "I am Dinbalo," which means in the Sidamo language, "One who keeps covered."

Another blind man regained his vision when twenty-nine evil spirits were evicted.

All of the following received healing for their minds: Noah Gonnes, who lost his reason for seven years; Nigatu Gobaro, for four years; Alemity Abebe, for six years; Nekia Gassim, for seven years; Conso Gobelle, for four years; Marta Solomon, for three years; and Befekadu Urano, for six years. Their families tried in vain to find help. Jesus did it! All of them gratefully serve the Lord.

Brother Gabiso Nonbers took his three-year-old son to a doctor, who pronounced the child dead. He then took the dead child to church, and by the prayer of faith, God raised him from the dead.

Pastor Eyob's brother crawled for twenty-five years with withered legs. When the amen concluded a prayer, he stood and walked on fully restored limbs. He received the better gift of salvation and has faithfully worked for the Lord ever since.

The doctors sent a man home to die after four years of treatment that did not help a painful problem which caused his stomach to swell excessively. He went to church for prayer and walked out well and a new creation in Christ.

Tadelech, sister-in-law of Erkenesh, developed brain cancer. A biopsy sent to Norway returned with the prognosis that she would die within fifteen days. Her complete, instant healing brought salvation to that household.

During a special time of prayer and fasting, carriers brought six palsied and paralyzed people from a distant village on homemade wooden stretchers. Four men were required to carry each makeshift cot. A wave of healing swept over them as the church united in prayer, and all six arose, perfectly whole. After church they chopped up the stretchers for a fire to make coffee!

During a revival at Worancha, many demon-tormented folks received liberty in the name of Jesus. The most unusual one was a man who had shrunken, blind eyeballs sunk deep into his head and distorted lips. His upper lip stretched to his right ear, and his lower lip stretched to the left ear. He looked like a hopeless monster. He had been force-fed with liquids for a year to keep him alive.

He was led screaming to Tekle, who immediately took dominion over the devil. Everyone watched his lips slowly return to normal. Tears began to roll down his face as the power of God restored his eyes to their proper place with perfect vision. God continues to move in astounding ways in the Sidamo region.

The Lord called Dawit Toshe, a second-year engineering student at the university, to take the gospel to his home district, Wollayta. He felt led to begin in the capital city of Soddo. Birhanu and Mengistu, two students, gave him tithes of four birr a month from their part-time employment and tried to help him however they could. The money barely kept him alive as he struggled to begin a church.

Persecution came repeatedly. His peers accused him to officials of hindering the progress of the country by giving up his education. They taunted him constantly for wasting brainpower by preaching, and their charges frequently sent him to jail. But Dawit had a vision of God's plan to establish churches in his area, and nothing turned him away from his goal. Later, the Lord gave him a dedicated wife, Emote, who was the pastor of a church before her marriage. (Under the leadership of Lencha, ten churches have come from that one.)

With only small assistance, Dawit and his helpers built a splendid place of worship. The church organization that opposed them with false charges and had them thrown in prison has since had all seven hundred of its churches closed permanently.

Four older preachers who accepted the truth earlier—Alaro, Debissa, Asha, and Datta Garano—work in beautiful harmony with their youthful presbyter, Dawit.

God Sends Revival

Debissa supervises thirteen churches that he won to the truth.

The two students who supported Dawit in the beginning are now pastors of churches, and more than eleven thousand have been born again, by water and Spirit, in Wollayta.

While Dawit preached at Eddo, a lady named Almaz left the service feeling ill and died a few minutes later. When Dawit heard the lamentation for the dead, he cut his sermon short and went to her house. "Do not be disturbed," he comforted her family. "God will bring her back from the dead."

Within thirty minutes she sat up and told how angels in white robes took her to heaven; then they said, "The people are praying for you. We will take you back."

Debena witnessed to Lemamo, who had suffered much from satanic attacks. He did not waste any time but was baptized in the name of Jesus that day and received the Holy Ghost. His furious wife put poison in his milk, and he became deathly ill. When Lemamo realized what had happened, he called on Jesus with all of his might. He vomited the poisoned milk and felt fine.

An extremely poisonous snake bit Bekle Deba, the assistant pastor in Abela. Usually, a person only has a few minutes to live when this venom enters his system. Though his leg swelled, his prayer in the name of Jesus spared his life. Dawit came that way a few days later, anointed the leg with oil, and prayed. The swelling disappeared instantly.

Genetu Gelasew, a pharmacist and pastor of an A.C.E. church, came with a sad story. His twelve-year-old son and fourteen-year-old daughter both lay seriously sick at home. Would Brother Dawit come and pray for them? Dawit had commitments he could not postpone, so he anointed handkerchiefs and prayed over them. "Lay these cloths on the children, and they will be healed," he said. When Genetu came home, he found his son well and playing normally. He laid a handkerchief on his daughter, and she received instant healing.

Later, Genetu's oldest daughter had such difficulty in labor that the clinic sent her home without hope; they did not have the skill or the equipment to help her. The baby arrived dead, choked by the cord. Brother Genetu prayed while the neighbors mocked him for praying over a dead child. After prayer, he turned the baby upside down and spanked him; he began to breathe and cried. God touched the mother, and she recovered quickly. The mockers had to give tribute to the mighty name of Jesus.

Aster Fiku traveled for five days to the health center, which could do nothing to help her. She asked her family to call Dawit. He could not come but sent an anointed handkerchief to lay on her stomach. When the cloth touched her, she went into a deep sleep for four hours. When Aster awakened, she easily gave birth to a healthy baby.

Genuine apostolic revival had come to the ancient land of Ethiopia.

God Sends Revival

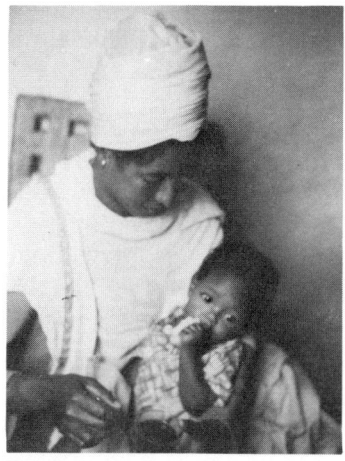

Tadelech, healed of a malignant brain tumor.

Invalid for 16 years healed.

Mamo and his family; tallest girl was healed of paralyzed legs.

Unseen Hands

Preachers in training.

Conference, 15,000 attended without a bench or a bed.

16

The Lord Working with Them

Tekle had won three churches to the truth in the Kambata District on one of his earlier tours. Addisse Tumeddedo traveled through the region with sound doctrine in word, song, and witness in 1975 and won thousands of souls. Many preachers joined the ranks, and this alarmed the S.I.M. and Lutheran leaders enough to make charges against them to the local police. This did not deter the preachers much; they went in and came out of jail rejoicing, time and again.

The church officials decided to take their complaints to the district administrator. "These men of the Apostolic church are winning our people to their belief," they accused.

"How do they persuade them to join their church?" the official questioned.

"With the Bible."

"Well, why don't you win them back with the Bible?"

the administrator asked. "Do you want me, an unbeliever, to do your work for you?" End of interview!

Miracles opened doors. A brother attended a funeral held at a home. In the lull before taking the deceased woman to the place of burial, he felt impressed of the Lord to pray for her. While he prayed she opened her eyes and asked, "Where have I been?" Sadness turned to happiness over that dramatic turnaround, which resulted in three pastors and their members receiving the Holy Ghost and being baptized in the name of Jesus.

Haile Limore from Ajarana Village was the president of the Lutheran young people for the whole region of Kambata. His friend Fakre Fusse gave him a book by Tekle called *New Birth*. Fakre had received the Holy Ghost while reading the booklet, and it led his friend to born-again salvation, too. Haile lost many material benefits in exchange for the truth, but he has made a tremendous impact on the youth of Kambata, winning many of them to righteousness. He has composed three hundred remarkable songs on doctrinal truths that have blessed the hearers.

Ambesse, a middle-aged man, abruptly became insane and for fifteen years was a worrisome nuisance to his wife and six children. No one could communicate with him, but several believers felt they should witness to him. He surprised them by listening, and in a very short time, the Lord restored his mind and saved him.

In Kidigisa Village, Dijamo, a nineteen-year-old young man, liked to sing in the choir and to serve the Lord. As time went by, he neglected to pray and read the Word and became lukewarm. Without warning, one day his whole body became paralyzed. He lay staring upward with

The Lord Working with Them

unseeing eyes and seemed not to hear anything spoken to him. Eight days of injections at the hospital availed nothing, and his parents brought him home.

His pastor returned from a journey on the twelfth day of his illness and came to pray for him. He called his name, "Dijamo! Dijamo!" then forced two fingers between his teeth to touch his tongue, saying, "Tongue, it is written that you must speak."

Dijamo regained consciousness and asked, "Who are you? Do not touch me if you have not been baptized in Jesus' name."

"I am your pastor—Elias. What happened to you?"

Dijamo confessed that he had grown cold in the Lord. "It felt as if two dragons had coiled around my neck and were going to kill me, but an angel slew them and saved my life." All of the churches took Dijamo's story as a warning that backsliding is dangerous.

Teshome Gebeyehu from the town of Hagere-Mariam in Sidamo Province heard of Tekle and his message. He came to see him in Awasa in 1972 to be baptized in the name of Jesus, and he received the Holy Ghost. After a few days he went home with a copy of Tekle's book *Divine Power*. Two years later he went to his home town, Chole, and by the book and his witness he led his three brothers and a nephew to the truth. He baptized them in Jesus' name and purposed to visit Tekle again to learn more.

He only knew that Tekle lived in Addis; he went to find him without knowing his address. He did not know the ways of the city either, and robbers took everything he had. That did not discourage him. Fasting, he walked up and down the streets for a week before he found his friend. Tekle expounded the Word to him until he felt better qualified to declare the gospel in his home village. He left Tekle with a request to visit his newly baptized relatives in Chole.

Wolde-Giorgis went with Tekle to Chole. Asefa, one of Teshome's brothers, received them as if they had been angels. They spent the night in teaching and praying. They baptized four the next day and six the day after that. The ten people baptized received their Spirit baptism before Tekle left for Addis, taking Asefa with him.

In Addis, they spent several days in intensive Bible study to prepare Asefa for the ministry, and Tekle sent him home ordained as pastor at Chole. The group grew until they could qualify for a land grant. They made application for one in January 1976.

The Coptic church relentlessly wielded its power to deny the Apostolics a place to bury their dead. In the few towns where people could dig graves on their own property, they were able to escape the Coptic threat "We will not give you a place to bury your loved ones unless you denounce the Apostolics."

In Chole the law required all graves to be on church property. Asefa and his believers praised God for a grant of eighteen thousand square yards, ample space for a church building and a cemetery. They learned of the extreme animosity held against their faith by the state church when they tried to bury a lady on their land. When they escorted the body to its last resting place, a mob surrounded them and someone began shooting into the crowd of believers. The police arrested Dejenne, who had come from the nearby town of Nazareth to help with the funeral, on the Coptic priest's word that he was the leader of the heretics.

The Lord Working with Them

In the midst of the confusion someone called the district administrator.

"All right," he said. "If you do not want them to bury their people on their own land, let the lady be buried at the Coptic church." The Coptics certainly would not agree to that, so he ordered them to leave the Apostolics alone and released Dejenne.

Asefa and his two brothers, Merru and Aberra, jointly owned a large shop that caught fire one night. Out of spite, the neighbors did not notify the owners, nor did they attempt to put out the fire. They said, "God is punishing them." The brothers praised the Lord for the loss of property valued at over sixty thousand birr and remained strong in the faith.

Chole had neither a hospital nor a clinic for Merru's wife to attend when she went into painful labor, and the child could not be born. She had not had this problem with any of her other children. The Coptics taunted, "Where is your God now?" The saints fasted and prayed. When it seemed she would die, the Lord touched her, and after a week of intense suffering, the baby came.

A group of fanatics called the town together, saying, "These people are heretics, and God will punish us if we do not destroy them." With many words of hate they stirred the mob to action. Priests, monks, and church leaders helped to fan their anger. The police brought the whole church to stand in the middle of the crowd to decide their fate. They had previously discussed what to do: should the "heretics" be executed in mass or dismembered or tortured? Now the mob was to make the decision.

The meek-looking group of saints prayed some unusual prayers that those surrounding them could not hear: "Lord, we rebuke Satan in the name of Jesus." "Jesus, send Your angel to bind this mob in Your name." "Let the angel of the Lord take action against these ungodly men and deliver Your children, in Your name, Jesus."

Something happened to the crowd. They stood motionless, almost as if they held their breath. No one spoke. "Come on," a leader scolded. "Speak up. Tell us what to do with them."

Half an hour of stony silence went by, then a priest tried to stand to make a recommendation, but something seemed to be holding him down. Finally, with supreme effort he got on his feet, but when he tried to open his mouth, he fell to the ground choking and gasping. The crowd fled in terror, confessing, "It looks as if the angel of the Lord is fighting for them; this must be the hand of God." They took the priest to the hospital, where he remained unable to speak for six months. The saints marched home with joy, singing a song of victory.

They only had the privilege of worshiping in their new sanctuary for four months before authorities seized it for a needed kindergarten. The parents of the town rebelled; they would not let their children be defiled by going where the Apostolics had worshiped. Asefa appealed again for burial ground, and the officials returned the land to the church.

A large group of people decided to attack the church during a service. They came armed with a fearful variety of weapons and planned to surround the church completely so that no one could escape. No one has told what they saw as they approached the church, but something put such terror in them that they could not get away fast

The Lord Working with Them

enough. That night the priest who organized the attack had a visitor. He reported that an angel appeared to him and said, "I am Gabriel, and I have come to tell you to stop fighting these people." One ringleader became insane before the night ended, and another one died in agony.

While death and sorrow came to their opponents, life reigned among the people of God. Adefris and Mestawet had only one child. A mule kicked the boy in the head, crushing his skull until his brain ruptured on one side. He died immediately, and many came to the funeral. Mestawet took the body in her arms and called on the Lord Jesus to raise him from the dead. Life returned and he became normal and well. A deep scar on his head will witness as long as he lives of the miracle God performed.

Through all of these things, the Lord added new souls to the church. In 1984, the administrator of the district decided to take matters in his own hand. He gave the people of Chole the right to rob, beat, and kill the Apostolics and burn their homes. He advertised this for many days, but the citizens of Chole had had enough. They refused to lift a finger against the church. This infuriated him, so he put the three leading men of the church in jail. On the third night he saw an angel of enormous stature and with a stern face standing before him. Few men have been so thankful to see the light of another day. He hurried to the prison, humbly apologized to the men, and released them. The church continues to march from victory to victory in Chole.

Later in 1974, Dejenne took charge of the churches in the Nazareth area and rented a house for seventy birr for services in the town.

Between 1975 and 1978, the five disfellowshipped national board members built a church in Nazareth with some of the money they had wrongfully kept from Brother Harris and the church. They sent one of the five, Ashenafi Andarge, to be pastor of this work. He struggled without making much progress until 1978, when the Lord appeared to him and told him that he would die if he did not repent and make things right with Tekle.

Shortly after the painful ministers meeting that ended with the final split in 1975, Amare had written a four-page letter to Brother T. F. Tenney, then director of foreign missions, accusing Tekle as a heretic who constantly worked against the United Pentecostal Church. He declared firmly that he, Amare, and his co-workers were the true followers of the doctrines of the church and that they would be faithful to the United Pentecostal Church but that Brother Tenney must take action against Tekle as he was not worthy to be a part of this great church.

Brother Tenney, according to standard office procedure, sent a copy of the letter to Brother Harris, who in turn sent a copy to Tekle, the recognized leader of the work.

When Ashenafi came repenting in 1978, he went all the way. He notified the government office dealing with property that the church actually belonged to the Apostolic Church of Ethiopia under the supervision of Reverend Teklemariam Gezahagne. (He could do this for the church had been built in his name.) Rejoicing, the saints in Nazareth moved out of the rented house into their own property.

Upon hearing this Amare wrote to the authorities that

The Lord Working with Them

Tekle actually belonged to a secret, subversive organization which the late emperor had expelled from Ethiopia, called the United Pentecostal Church. He expressed shock that his building valued at 150,000 birr should be given to the local agent, Teklemariam, to be used for seditious programs under the guise of religion.

His letter made the rounds of the offices that investigated such matters, and the authorities summoned Tekle to bring his defense against Amare's charges. Tekle sent Ashenafi to the office with a copy of Amare's letter to Brother Tenney. When the authorities read the letter they called in Amare. "So you are the follower of this secret organization, the United Pentecostal Church, and not Teklemariam as you have charged." They cleared Tekle of all blame and released Amare with two serious warnings: he must never lay claim to the church in Nazareth again, and if they ever found out that the United Pentecostal Church was involved in any political affairs, they would hold him responsible and he would suffer the consequences.

The church in Nazareth moves steadily on, and Tekle treasures the verses of Scripture the Lord gave him at that time.

"Behold, he that keepeth Israel shall neither slumber nor sleep" (Psalm 121:4).

"But now thus saith the LORD that created thee... Fear not: for I have redeemed thee, I have called thee by thy name; thou art mine. When thou passest through the waters, I will be with thee; and through the rivers, they shall not overflow thee: when thou walkest through the fire, thou shalt not be burned; neither shall the flame kindle upon thee. For I am the LORD thy God, the Holy

One of Israel, thy Saviour: I gave Egypt for thy ransom, Ethiopia and Seba for thee. Since thou wast precious in my sight, thou hast been honourable, and I have loved thee: therefore will I give men for thee, and people for thy life" (Isaiah 43:1-4).

Twenty-seven more churches have been established in that district.

A personal crisis followed the victory. Two-year-old Jerusalem had measles with complications that caused her death. While Erkenesh wept in the bathroom, Tekle lay on the floor praying. After two hours, God restored life, but her sightless eyes could not focus. Tekle continued to pray. In a short while, scales fell from her eyes. Today, Jerusalem is a lovely, soft-spirited girl with unusually bright eyes.

Truly Mark 16:20 is being fulfilled today in Ethiopia: "And they went forth, and preached every where, the Lord working with them, and confirming the word with signs following."

Presbyter of Kambata with family; smallest child was raised from the dead.

The Lord Working with Them

Building a country church.

Dijamo – raised from the dead.

Part of 600 on the way to the baptismal water.

Unseen Hands

The Tenneys in front of the miracle building.

Lunchtime. 82 preachers were ordained at the dedication.

Dedicating the headquarters church at Addis.

17

Advancing in the Name of Jesus

The one-to-one concept of evangelism, learned in perilous times, served the church well. Expansion came so rapidly that Tekle had a difficult time keeping up with the necessary teaching, training, and instruction so that babes in Christ could learn to discern between evil and good. He regularly expresses his gratitude for the anointed ministry of three men closely associated with the work in Ethiopia: John Harris, Donald Ikerd, and E. L. Freeman. "I could not have made it without them," he declares.

Young men were sent to Life Tabernacle Bible School in Kenya and returned after graduation to bless the work with untiring assistance. Branches of the churches in Addis worshiped in homes and under trees, encouraged by faithful men, especially Dawit, Degu, and Tebebe. Then came the government's ultimatum: "Stop meeting in homes! We will no longer allow churches to meet in

Unseen Hands

private dwellings."

Tekle consulted with Brother Harris, who answered, "I don't know, Brother Tekle. If we build, the building may be nationalized, and we would lose everything. I'll pray about it." After discussions with the regional field supervisor, who added his supplication to theirs, they felt a go-ahead signal from the Lord and began raising funds.

Backed by considerable prayer and fasting and encouraged by God's promise that his request would receive a favorable answer, Tekle had applied for a land grant in August 1976. He was told, "We will consider your request for a place to build a church when you produce a bank statement showing that you have at least fifty thousand birr in the bank." He did not have a bank account, much less any money, so back home he went for more days of fasting and prayer!

During this time Tekle suffered from acute asthma for three years, and Erkenesh prayed earnestly and constantly for a better house, away from an open sewer. God spoke to her one day: Do not pray for your own house; pray for a headquarters church building. She joined Tekle in his petitions to the throne.

Tekle returned to the government office to check on his application, and they sent him to the surveyor's office. He found his application form there with this notation: "It has been agreed to grant the Apostolic Church of Ethiopia an appropriate plot of land for the erection of a church building." This was a miracle, considering that numerous churches had been closed and many suffered restrictions!

The surveyor asked for the design of a building costing at least 100,000 birr. Architects wanted to charge

Advancing in the Name of Jesus

1,500 for the blueprints, but the surveyor agreed to make the drawing for 500. With the completion of the plan, Tekle could give him only 200 birr—all that he had. When they realized the unsuitability of the design, architecture students Tesfaye Adefres and Solomon Ketema drew blueprints that the municipality accepted, and they did not charge for their work.

Tekle had no assurance of finance for the church other than God's promise, and innumerable obstacles surfaced to hinder the work. The church learned again that prayer and fasting can handle anything. Limited means did not stop the saints from giving sacrificially for the building; by faith, even those existing on the edge of starvation gave beyond their nonexistent resources. Brothers Harris and Freeman asked the Louisiana District to help, and the late Brother C. G. Weeks raised $23,000 to apply on the project. Brother Scism, director of foreign missions, supported the venture.

Erkenesh no longer prayed for a home, but Brother Harris saw the need, and God moved on him to help build a parsonage next to the new church. The same loving hands that constructed the church pitched in to give Tekle and Erkenesh their first decent home. Brother Harris strained the budget and his ingenuity to help with furnishings. Tekle's asthma and Mehret's chronic bronchitis both disappeared within days after they moved into the new parsonage and finally got away from the sewer's noxious fumes.

Spiritual descendants of Sanballat (who opposed Nehemiah's rebuilding of Jerusalem) hurried to government offices with petitions and objections from the minute Tekle started building a wall around the property. One of them who had wide influence was arrested on the way for misappropriation of government funds. All the rest heard no for an answer.

The children of the Lord had a mind to work. Bekele was employed in an office but spent his free time helping to dig the foundation. Tewolde, Tekle's younger brother and an efficient mason, did the floors and similar work. Ayele Lakew, Salome's grandson and pastor of the Addis church, handled the electrical and telephone installations. Preachers and members skilled in masonry and carpentry came from Wollayta and Chole. These and others working together saved forty percent of the construction costs. As the work progressed the services were moved—first to the service quarters, then to the living room of the parsonage.

The first meeting in the unfinished church was held on the Ethiopian Christmas Day, January 7, 1980. A spirit of giving moved over the congregation, and they piled on the platform a great stack of watches, clothes, and other valuables. These contributions helped to finish the sanctuary.

Huge crowds gathered on August 30, 1980, for the dedication of the church to the memory of the late C. G. Weeks. Brother Tenney preached a powerful dedicatory message that will never be forgotten by those present. His prayer of dedication has been a pivot of faith when storms have threatened. It is quoted and reprayed word for word with all of its original fervency: "To the message of truth we dedicate this church; we dedicate these men; we dedicate these saints. We officially give this building and ourselves to Jesus; from now on this building belongs to Him. I have no claim on this building; the people of

Advancing in the Name of Jesus

Louisiana and you who have contributed money here have no claim on it. It is God's; it is God's!"

The believers melted together in worship of Jesus, who gives victory to His church regardless of the circumstances. Sister Tenney, Sister Bobbye Wendell, Brother and Sister John Harris and Brother Freeman came to share in the exuberant celebration.

The Lord graciously restored the saints who fell away in 1975, and revival spread from Addis to adjacent suburbs and towns. At Debre-Zeit, a young man who was grotesquely disfigured by cancer that covered most of his body received a healing touch from the Great Physician, who not only healed and saved him but also restored him to a pleasing appearance. Two insane people, a woman with breast cancer, a girl with devastating asthma, a young woman dying with tuberculosis, and numbers of demon-possessed people received healing, restoration, and the gift of life. The list goes on and on, because the power of Jesus is unlimited.

I came to Addis again for a visit in 1983. It had been seven years since I had had that privilege. As Tekle gave Brother Freeman the annual progress reports in the parsonage, I heard sweet singing from the nearby church and could hardly wait to get there. Finally, Tekle closed the colossal books containing the most detailed records I have ever seen.

"Let's go to church," he invited.

An unprecedented force flowed over us as we walked approximately fifty yards to the side entrance of the packed edifice. I turned to my husband and asked, "Do you feel something?"

He smiled, "I feel the presence of God flowing like

a river!"

"That's it!" I felt inundated by a holy richness of the Spirit that I had never experienced before. I floated into the church and huddled in a corner on the platform, needing to talk to my Friend.

"Dearest Jesus, the matchless charge of Your supernatural love swirling around me is so dynamic and electrifying, and yet the very depth of my soul glows in Your satisfying embrace. I thank You, but I do not understand what is happening. Would it be Your will to explain this beautiful phenomenon to me?"

I waited quietly, while the precious Ethiopians worshiped in holy abandon.

My answer came: Child, for the first time in your life you are in the presence of perfect unity. Having been stripped of hope, rank, wealth, and often even decency, these hearts have joined together as *one* heart to magnify My name. I pour my blessings on unity.

The Book of Acts was duplicated in that service: we saw demons cast out, the afflicted made whole, and the spiritually hungry filled with bread from heaven. The service was not arranged by human design or intelligence; living water flowed with easy sweetness as orchestrated by the Holy Ghost.

On the organizational side, the national church office issued credentials and identity cards, kept records, and added stability to the work. The body of believers reached out with an extensive ministry of tracts, tapes, books, and Bible studies. The headquarters church sponsors evangelists who go everywhere, "with signs following." They are determined to multiply the revival in Ethiopia until Jesus comes again.

Advancing in the Name of Jesus

Growth of the Apostolic Church of Ethiopia

The following graph shows the believers, churches, and preachers added to the A.C.E. each year from 1975 to 1986.

Year	Baptized in Jesus' name	Holy Ghost filled	Churches added	Preachers added
1975	6,086	7,560	24	24
1976	7,156	7,156	5	5
1977	6,489	8,950	10	10
1978	8,156	5,119	10	10
1979	9,337	3,675	5	10
1980	9,296	7,500	9	35
1981	8,213	7,875	37	35
1982	18,330	10,330	28	41
1983	7,970	7,969	141	100
1984	8,821	8,517	55	145
1985	14,648	6,568	56	61
1986	8,756	5,756	128	128
Total	113,258	86,975	508	604

It should be noted that many of those baptized in Jesus' name had already received the Holy Ghost before coming into the A.C.E., which explains much of the disparity between the first two columns.

There are 488 preaching places in addition to the established churches. "Ethiopia shall soon stretch out her hands unto God" (Psalm 68:31).

Unseen Hands

The visitors.

Gifts from the Ethiopian church at the dedication.

All preachers conference.

Advancing in the Name of Jesus

Tekle's family.

Mehret on her wedding day.

Unseen Hands

Paralyzed man healed at Kambata.

The church is too small!

18

The End Is Not Yet

Erkenesh went deep into the valley at the birth of her last child. Tekle returned from another conference in Jerusalem to find her suffering in great pain. Before he could change clothes a messenger came with the sad news of the death of Tamru, Erkenesh's oldest brother. Since she could not possibly travel to Kambata, a distance of 350 kilometers, Tekle had no choice but to accompany the messenger in her place. He returned three days later, and fifteen days later, on December 24, 1981, Yasu (Joshua) was born into the family. They chose his name to show their faith in and anticipation of the heavenly Canaan.

Under the considerate leadership of John Harris, the church in Ethiopia and her leaders cherished a Jonathan-David relationship with him. He is remembered for tremendous sermons, fourteen church buildings that he helped to build (four of them major projects), numerous gifts of love, and delivering Tekle from taxis! The mature Opel he obtained for Tekle is a wonder car—a series of

Unseen Hands

constant miracles keeps it going.

During Brother Harris's administration, the A.C.E. learned the high value of unity, and that close harmony with the missionaries and leaders of the church paid a rich dividend of revival. They have not forgotten.

God's will sent John Harris home in 1982, and the Foreign Missions Division selected Brother Freeman as the new superintendent of Ethiopia. In God's order, one person is not an exact replacement of another in a church leadership position, but each person must fill his post as Jesus leads. Enthusiastic cooperation has made the superintendency a never failing joy. When Erkenesh and Tekle heard of the appointment, they declared, "Ethiopia will be blessed abundantly, not only by Brother Freeman walking in our land, but also with the words of his mouth."

For three years, each time she prayed, Erkenesh heard herself repeating over and over, "Jemjem, Jemjem, Jemjem!" She wondered what the word meant. Only later did she learn that it was the name of a place where God triggered a holy chain reaction that exploded in revival and persecution. God directed her to Isaiah 65:1: "I am sought of them that asked not for me; I am found of them that sought me not: I said, Behold me, behold me, unto a nation that was not called by my name."

In 1983 three Lutheran churches held a joint, one-day conference in Guji in the Jemjem area. While a preacher prayed for the congregation laboriously according to their custom, suddenly an unprecedented spirit of prayer and praise fell on the listeners, surprising them all. As the people shouted, danced, leaped, and spoke in tongues, the three pastors went outside to discuss this strange situation. A student from the Apostolic church

The End Is Not Yet

came by, recognized the sound from heaven coming from inside the church, and explained the Scriptures to the preachers.

He offered to take them to the Apostolic presbyter of Alata-Wondo, one hundred kilometers away, who could teach them more. They went, were taught by Zerihun, received the baptism of both water and Spirit, returned to tell their churches what had happened to them, and told the people what they should do. Zerihun came and baptized six hundred people in the name of Jesus in one day.

The same wonderful, simultaneous outpouring of the Holy Ghost came to sixteen Lutheran churches as the Apostolic preachers witnessed to them. Nineteen Apostolic churches were now in the region with 3120 born-again members. Godana Haro became presbyter of Jemjem and Borana provinces.

Tekle came to America for the first time in 1984 to attend the general conference in Anaheim, California. On the second day he told me his wife had gone to Jemjem District for a conference and should be home by then, but no one answered the phone at their home in Addis.

"Keep trying, Tekle," I said. "You need to hear from her."

I watched him worship in the service that night and thought, No one would guess that the threat of a serious problem is hanging over his head.

No news came the next day.

He came to me the following morning and said calmly, "I have learned that my wife is in jail in Kebre-Mengist in Jemjem."

I called Brother Freeman out of a board meeting to

discuss the emergency. "Tekle, we can get you on the next plane to Ethiopia," he suggested.

"No," Tekle answered with a faraway look in his eyes. "If I could talk to her, I'm sure she would say, 'Finish the work you went to America to do, but *pray!*' Please help me pray. Jesus is still our deliverer."

I watched Tekle's reaction in the next service. With eyes closed and a smile of pure joy on his face he danced, leaped, pranced, and ran around the auditorium while he spoke and sang in a heavenly language. He did not slack or waver in worship for the rest of the conference, and I learned another lesson about trust and praise.

After the conference, Tekle and Brother Freeman visited several churches to be a blessing and to raise necessary funds. He put everything he could into every service. The good news only came eighteen days later: "Erkenesh has been released."

We learned that Erkenesh went to Jemjem Province for a conference with Dejene, pastor at Nazareth, and his wife, Menbere. Because of accusations from a Lutheran church leader, the police arrested them at Bore, the town nearest the nineteen churches. Their accuser declared that the Apostolics taught people how to sin: "They even commit adultery at church."

No one would listen to their firm explanation: "We teach purity of heart and holiness." They were taken to jail in Kibre-Mengist, a neighboring town.

The next morning their accuser galloped away toward the country, and his horse threw him. He died with a crushed skull that spilled his brains on the ground. One of his colleagues brought nine more believers to jail and jumped on his horse to go burn down an Apostolic church.

The End Is Not Yet

His horse stumbled and he died on the spot.

Crammed in an airless room for a week without a bed, a chair, light, water or food, the ladies suffered from ants that had the right-of-way on the dirt floor and bit them constantly. The saints came with food, and the prisoners felt the assurance of their love, but Erkenesh said that she did not once feel the presence of the Lord in the prison. "I continued to pray and to praise Jesus, though my heart seemed dry and cold and I could not feel Him."

Guards moved the ladies to a roofless verandah where they shivered under their wet blankets and were repeatedly doused by the cold rain.

"If you had a sheep out in the rain, would you not take it to shelter?" Erkenesh asked one of them. "Are we not more valuable than sheep?"

He snarled his answer. "You Pentes! You are destroying our country."

Erkenesh discerned that like Felix with Paul, he wanted money. The guards came to the ladies frequently with evil designs, but they could not break through the power of the name of Jesus.

The police, encouraged by church leaders, did everything possible to discredit and harass the church. To torment them, they brought a mutilated body to the ladies, saying, "Look at this poor man! The Apostolics killed him!"

One guard went to a pastor and said, "We are going to kill all of the religious people except your folks. Give us their names and addresses so they will be spared." They took the addresses and those they got from Erkenesh's notebook and planned a diabolical scheme to wipe out the church.

Unseen Hands

Officials at a high level said, "No! This church is not subversive; Tekle is a helpful man. Scrap these plans."

Although the local authorities had jailed only twelve people, for months they had spread many rumors: "All of the Pentes are in jail!" "Tekle is dead!" "Tekle embezzled millions of birr and fled to Nairobi. We caught him and have brought him back to prison!"

The people answered, "Our faith is not built on Teklemariam. Our faith is built on Jesus, and we will not deny Him."

After two weeks on the verandah, Menbere persuaded a guard to take her to a telephone, and a call to a prestigious friend brought about their release.

A vicious man burned the church at the village of Murri where Godana was pastor. The believers prayed in the ashes and began building another church. The arsonist went on a trip and burned three more churches located in other villages. He became furious when he returned and saw that the believers had rebuilt the church at Murri, so he decided to burn the new church, too.

Then an invisible fire made his flesh so hot that no one could bear to touch him. He screamed, "The God of the Apostolics is burning me because I burned His churches!" He screamed and cried for fifteen days before he died, and his family had to pour water continually on his burning body. They covered him with wet clothes and wet leaves in order to bury him. Many of the spectators came to repentance, crying to God for mercy, which He graciously gave.

An armed band came to the village of Denbeb and killed the livestock of the believers. They prepared themselves a feast, then beat the saints in an effort to

The End Is Not Yet

force them to drink brandy. Suddenly, a rival band came on the scene and fired into the crowd, leaving twelve of the agitators dead and several wounded. The injured saw that none of God's children had been hurt and realized the wrong they had done. They began to repent and were baptized, strengthening the church at Denbeb.

An angel opened the door to the village of Borre in Jemjem Province. He appeared to Lotu, who had been sick for all of her eight years, and said, "If you will believe in the name of Jesus you will be healed. Have nothing to do with the idols of your witch doctor Moslem father. Do not believe as your parents do; obey them only in matters that are good and right, and you will be the child of God."

She told her parents what had happened the next day. They saw plainly the effect of the healing touch but could not understand what had happened.

Her father held a high position as chief of all the witch doctors, and he announced a great celebration in honor of their many idols. He sent Lotu and her younger sister to the river to bring water for the heathen sacrifices. Three angels met them, and one spoke to Lotu. "Did I not tell you to have nothing to do with idolatry?" Hearing his word, Lotu fell to the ground as one lifeless. Her frightened little sister ran sobbing to tell their parents what had happened.

Word spread rapidly through the town, and the whole village came to see what had happened to Lotu. By this time she had received the Holy Ghost, and they found her rejoicing in other tongues. She immediately warned them not to come too near. "This is holy ground, for Jesus is here. Do not touch me with your defiled hands that have sacrificed to idols. You cannot be clean until you believe in Jesus, the only God."

While she witnessed with amazing boldness, a young lady from an Apostolic church happened to pass by on her way to visit another village. Listening as the young child spoke with Holy Ghost anointing and realizing what had happened, she interrupted to ask the crowd if they would accept an evangelist from her church who would tell them more about God's plan of salvation.

They agreed. The evangelist came quickly, and people who had never heard the truth before accepted God's Word with genuine repentance. Lotu and nineteen others were baptized that day, and they burned twenty Korans before sunset.

In the next few weeks, many others followed their example. The Lord sent them a pastor. Fifty more ex-Moslems burned their Korans, and a strong church blossomed at Borre.

A church sectional leader watched the growth of the new church with alarm. He first fought it with malicious slander and denied the scriptural passages about baptism in the name of Jesus and the baptism of the Holy Ghost. This only fanned the fire, so he decided to take drastic action. He went to the pastor's home with a machine gun and shot into the house seventy times. Neither the house nor its occupants showed a mark from the attack.

Then he decided to outshine them. He built an impressive building, prepared a bountiful feast, and invited many distinguished guests. While still at home, in the midst of helpers and guests, lightning struck and killed him. No one could touch his body, for the blue fire of lightning enveloped him from head to foot. The mourners

The End Is Not Yet

waited for hours for the body to cool so that it could be buried, but it did not. Finally, European missionaries went to a larger town to get some insulation material. With that they eventually were able to place the body in the ground. From that day, the whole countryside exalted the name of Jesus and the church expanded freely.

Conference time for Jemjem Province had been planned in a church near Borre in August 1986. Because the building could not hold the three thousand people who came, the services were moved into the open air. Realizing the shortage of food, the leaders Degu (from Addis) and Godana (presbyter) declared, "This is a prayer and fasting conference."

Rich blessings flowed as a life-giving river, refreshing the believers throughout the conference to the closing service. Afterwards the believers started walking toward those faraway places they called home. A group of thirty new converts going to Murri were attacked by spear wielding gangsters. At first they tried to defend themselves, with little success; then a spirit of boldness came over them. They snatched the spears out of the hands of their attackers and sent them running. A little girl who was with them ran back to warn the preachers who were following to take another route home to avoid the gangsters.

That night the thirty gathered at Godana's house, stitched their wounds together with needles and thread (for there were no clinics in that remote area), and prayed the rest of the night. The dawn found every injury completely healed as if the stitching had been done several days before.

One miracle followed another, bringing healing and

Unseen Hands

deliverance to believers, and the judgment of God fell on the unruly and the disobedient until the message of truth reached the far corners of Jemjem and word spread to the neighboring province of Borana.

A young man named Tesfaye went to Borana to teach school. He witnessed to the pastor of a Lutheran church and his associates. They answered, "We have been warned against the Apostolics for five years and would like to know what you teach." The men had open and hungry hearts. After they heard Tesfaye, the senior pastor asked him to teach the whole congregation. Five hundred people received the Word and wanted to be baptized. Tesfaye took the pastor to Dawit, presbyter of Wollayta, who baptized him.

Dawit and Genetu went to Borana early in January and baptized 160 souls at midnight, for by this time great opposition had begun. The two brothers slipped away secretly to avoid arrest and disappointed more than three hundred who hoped to be baptized the next day. God saw their tears and hungry hearts and sent Brother Freeman in the third week of January to ordain their pastors and send them back to baptize their people.

Debena felt the call of God to go to the South to Wollayto. There he founded a church, was arrested, and was jailed for six months. Finally the government office where he worked sent him away so that he could not preach there anymore.

Debena's job transferred him to Jimma Province. To his surprise, he found three hundred Lutherans, and he began to teach them in private prayer meetings. (This was amazing because that area is largely pagan.) He began to explain the Word more fully to them, and they were filled with the Holy Ghost.

In the West, Debena witnessed to seven evangelists. They, along with many other Spirit-filled people, desired water baptism in Jesus' name. Debena took the evangelists to Addis for baptism, and while there, he and the evangelists received ordination.

They returned to the West, hoping to spread revival; instead they went to prison because of false reports to the police. Debena was released after six months. The seven preachers stayed longer before facing trial, though they could have been set free at any time by denying their salvation. The judge would only accept political charges that had nothing to do with religion, so he dismissed the men.

Revival came, and with it came much persecution. Debena's job made preaching illegal for him, but he did not stop, despite frequent warnings. The police arrested the eight men again, including Debena, and took them with their children and nursing babies to the capital city for "questioning." That consisted of making them kneel on the sand and beating them unmercifully every day for a week. Death loomed over them each day, but as they called on the name of Jesus, healing and strength came. . .so that they could return for another beating!

They returned home with harsh threats ringing in their ears, determined to preach the gospel as never before. The government fired Debena from his good job, and he rejoiced to be set free to work for the Lord. He is now presbyter of the western region and has reached to the Illubabor region, the border of Sudan, and the Anyuak tribal people.

In 1969, when Tekle and Erkenesh went to Negele

on their first evangelistic trip, the Holy Ghost fell at a Lutheran mission. Abebech was one of those who received the Spirit. In later contacts with Tekle, she began to understand the Word better and remained true to the doctrine under difficult circumstances.

Inspired by the moving account of the Israelites possessing their Canaan, Abebech staked her claim on that mission soon after being born again. She prayed daily with fervent faith, "Lord, give me my inheritance."

Since her husband worked for the mission, they lived in the mission compound. She found herself in trouble often and in jail frequently. Nothing fazed her or wilted her faith. She heard but did not heed warnings such as, "If you listen to the Apostolics, you will be attacked by the evil spirit that lives in them."

Forbidden to speak, Abebech sang explicit songs of doctrine to her children in a clear, loud voice so that everyone near her could not help but hear. After times of prayer and fasting, she declared boldly, "I will inherit this mission."

In 1987 God honored eighteen years of unwavering faith. First, thirty hostel students repented and requested baptism by immersion in the name of Jesus. Next, eight preachers and 250 church members obeyed the Word and walked in the light. The one remaining missionary decided to return to Europe because, he said, "The Apostolics have taken over the mission." Abebech inherited!

Yared was only sixteen years old in 1987, but he has chalked up a most remarkable record of soul winning. He had little opportunity for training in an established church since soon after his conversion his stepfather transferred to Meki. With holy zeal burning in his heart, Yared won

The End Is Not Yet

fifty Coptic believers and called Dejene to come and baptize them. After he arrived, authorities threw the candidates in jail as well as Dejene.

A two-month prison sentence did not change their convictions; Dejene baptized them when they got out. Their former leaders sent a supposedly holy replica of the ark to the homes of several prestigious families in an attempt to regain their confidence in ancient traditions. When that failed, they sent out a circular asking that Yared be killed on sight.

God protected him. His stepfather took a pistol to kill him, but he got away from him as David did from the angry King Saul. Then the stepfather hired an assassin. An angel awakened Yared three times during the night to show him the room's door that he had closed and locked each time standing wide open. The would-be murderer was foiled. While he waited for another chance to kill Yared, the police arrested the hired killer for attempted robbery.

Over two hundred believers worship the Father in spirit and in truth in that small town, and Yared is looking for more souls to win.

We heard a young evangelist, Fitsum Berhan, give a thrilling testimony on our visit to Ethiopia in 1986. He works for the Lord near the border, where war and turmoil is a way of life. He ignored several warnings to stop preaching. Caught again in the act, a commanding officer sent him to the forest to die before a firing squad. Looking over his executioners, he realized that they represented varied beliefs and backgrounds so he spoke with a clear voice, "Just before you shoot me, let me tell you about Jesus!"

Unseen Hands

The voices of the soldiers rose in a babble.
"Who's He?"
"The second person of the trinity."
"No, no, He is only a prophet."
"I have never heard of Him before."
"Well, he's the Son of God."
The discussion between Muslims, Orthodox, heathen, Satan worshipers, and many other religionists became so heated that Fitsum Berhan slipped away unnoticed.

That surprising scene had two reruns with different actors and different backgrounds but the same central character, proving that Jesus can tailor deliverance for His own.

Tekle's oldest daughter, Mehret, married the brave evangelist not long after we heard the incredible story of his three escapes, and we learned that there have been many others. May the unfailing Deliverer ever hold the young couple in His tender care at their lonely outpost.

Only the dazzling faith of the Apostolics of Ethiopia can account for the final three testimonies of this book, included on the insistence of Tekle and Erkenesh.

They believe that Brother Freeman and I bring a miracle when we visit them, and their uncomplicated faith makes it happen. Incessant prayers from the church bombarded heaven over the widely known drought that caused so many deaths. The Lord impressed Erkenesh in 1985 that if we prayed for rain, it would come. As we left their home for the airport, Tekle requested, "Please lift up your holy hands over our land that God may send us rain."

We stood on a slight elevation in the church grounds and prayed a simple prayer with uplifted hands. Four days later the rains began. Places where rain had not fallen

The End Is Not Yet

in six years (according to reports printed in the U.S.) received copious rains. Now crops are growing widely, providing food for the hungry.

Barriers and closed doors hindered the work of the Lord in 1986. A group photograph in front of the church after dismissal marked the end of a conference made glorious by the presence of the King. Just after we broke the pose, but before the group moved away, Tekle made a request. "The work of God is stymied. Churches are closed; we are not free to take the gospel where it should go; towns have barred us. Please ask God to open doors in the land for our preachers and to give them the courage and anointing to go through those doors."

We prayed and hurried to the airport to keep up with our usual stiff schedule. Down the road and far away, the report caught up with us of doors miraculously opened, of new boldness, and of men mightily anointed to do the will of God. All the barriers did not fall, but the Mighty One showed the church how to work around them with the landslide power of revival. After that prayer, six hundred Lutherans were baptized in four months in Negele.

Erkenesh felt grieved over the continuing border wars that cost dearly in the lives of men. She hated to see godly young men drafted from their churches to be dumped into the carnage of war. She thought, The Miracle of 1987 must be the end of the war. But this time they did not ask for us to pray; they only believed that it would happen because we came.

We cannot forget the glory of the preachers' conference. Hundreds of them came from distant places, bringing the glow of their dedication to brush our souls with angels' wings. A record 151 preachers received ordination. With their faces on the floor, trembling with tears of joy, they felt a shining anointing of God's Spirit hover over them. We all experienced the indescribable presence of the King of kings in a glory cloud that strengthened and prepared the new ministers for service.

Our souls enriched, we left Addis. In April 1987, when Erkenesh came briefly to bless the church in America, we learned about the miracle she had claimed.

"Jesus answered, but not the way I expected," she explained. "A fine young man from one of our churches who was drafted to fight felt so sad and discouraged that he went into the forest near his station to pray. He rolled on the ground in desperation, asking, 'O God, is this my place? What do I have to do with guns and fighting? I only want to work for You. I don't want to stay here. Help me, Lord!' He wept bitterly. At that very moment God sent a little bird that began to sing to him in his own language, 'Praise God! Praise God! Praise God!'

"Startled, he wiped away his tears and timidly began to praise the Lord with the bird as it sat on the low limb of a tree. As the soldier's praises gained momentum, they swept away self-pity and discouragement. He returned to camp full of joy and with a holy purpose to witness. In a very short time, thirteen communist soldiers repented and were baptized in the name of Jesus.

"You see," Erkenesh concluded, "God did not stop the war. He answered by sending a revival to save soldiers gathered from every province."

Miracles and revivals continue in Ethiopia, and the end is not yet. Praise the Lord!

Appendix

The Road to Ethiopia

by Michael L. Trapasso

The work of God in Ethiopia today is inextricably woven to the past. Part of that past is a pamphlet which God used to open the door to revival in Ethiopia. What follows is the amazing story of how the Lord brought that pamphlet into existence. It is not a tale of how God used a giant man of God: to the contrary, it is more akin to the old story about a shepherd boy with a few stones and a sling whom God used to bring about a great victory.

The First Battle Over My Baptism

"Give me my son. I'm taking him to the priest to have him baptized into the Catholic church." I was only a few days old when my Italian father made this demand of my mother. My poor mother, did not know what to do. No longer was she in the comfort and security of a Pentecostal family in the piney woods of East Texas. She was now living in Niagara Falls, New York, backslidden and alone.

Momentarily, my little ninety-pound, four-foot-eleven-inch mother resisted my father, but she knew that at any time he might overpower her and take me from her arms. But something arose inside her. She remembered the wonderful truth that her father, Reverend Leon Day, preached: salvation is in the name of Jesus, and baptism must be in that name.

My Mother's Offering

Mother also remembered the story of Hannah and how she offered her only son to God. Without a preacher, without a church, without any anointing oil, but with a sincere heart, she offered me—her only son—to God, utterly and completely. The Lord accepted my mother's offering and protected me from being baptized into the Catholic church. Soon thereafter we moved to Texas.

The Second Battle Over My Baptism

In the winter of 1961, some fourteen years later, Brother and Sister Wayne Trout preached a revival at the United Pentecostal Church in Beaumont, Texas, where Reverend R. D. Gibson was pastor. During this time, on February 11, 1961, I attended the meeting and found the Lord.

That night I went home and put my arms around my father, telling him that Jesus had baptized me with the Holy Ghost.

I never will forget my father's reaction. He said I was not his son any more, and the next day he left home.

Now a second battle over my baptism took place. My father, remembering my mother's refusal to allow me to be baptized into the Catholic church, drew the line. He said I was not to be baptized, and that if I was, he would not come home. I loved my father dearly. How I wanted

Appendix: The Road to Ethiopia

him to come home! But Jesus put me to the test, and even as a child, I found His words to be true: "He that loveth father and mother more than me is not worthy of me. . . .He cannot be my disciple" (Matthew 10:37; Luke 14:26).

The choice was made; I decided to follow Jesus. Arrangements were made for my baptism. On February 13, 1961, I was baptized into that wonderful life-giving name—the name of Jesus. My mother and sister, who were also baptized that day, were the only ones present besides Pastor Gibson.

Miraculous Manifestations

Something beautiful and miraculous happened when I was baptized. Although it was winter and we had no heated baptistery, the Spirit of the Lord came down, and I actually felt the water grow warm.

Soon Brother Gibson plunged me beneath the waters to be buried with Christ, dead to sin, dead to self, and raised up a new creature in Christ Jesus.

I then went into the back room by myself to change garments while my mother, my sister, and Brother Gibson waited in the front. At this time a second heavenly manifestation took place. Suddenly, I began to hear heavenly music that filled the air with great joy, music that was as audible as any I have ever heard. I looked above my head to see where it was coming from. Then the most glorious, heavenly sounds filled the room. I cannot fully explain it, but I fully experienced it. So sudden and so awesome was this manifestation that I fled from the room. Like the child Samuel I did not understand what God was doing.

Preparation in the Word

At the age of fourteen, then, I began a new life, a life in Christ Jesus. I knew so little of the things of God, but He soon remedied that. My grandmother gave me a thirty-nine-cent pocket New Testament. At the same time, the Lord gave me an instant love for His Word. I remember well the deep, deep hunger for His Word, a hunger that drove me to study that little Bible for six hours or more a day.

I felt compelled to take the little Bible to school. My father had returned home, but he forbade me to take my Bible to school. However, I just could not help but take it with me. Oh, what fellowship I enjoyed with Jesus and His Word! Often I would skip lunch so as to have more time to feed on the Word of God. Classmates would make fun of me as I sat by a tree reading the Bible, but that did not matter; nothing mattered but Jesus. In class I would read the Bible, after school I would read the Bible, late at night I would read that little Bible.

I did not understand this unquenchable, insatiable desire I had for the Word. In retrospect, I can see that the Lord was preparing me to write a pamphlet only five years later at the age of nineteen.

More Preparation

At age seventeen, my grammar was atrocious. On my first day in the tenth grade, my English teacher told the class to write an essay so that she could evaluate our ability to write. When my essay was graded and given back to me, on it was written in red ink a message I will never forget: "F--. If you can't do any better than this, I can't help you." Just twenty-four months later, I wrote the

Appendix: The Road to Ethiopia

pamphlet on baptism. During this interlude, the Lord prepared me by sending into my life perhaps the most gifted teacher I have ever known—an English teacher. She transformed me from an F-- student to at least an average one. To her, and to the Lord who sent her, I will always be grateful.

The Stage is Set

In the winter of 1966, Ovid Peterson, a sixteen-year-old Norwegian, took to the high seas. His parents were missionaries in Argentina. In his desire to support their work, he decided to work on a grain ship headed for the port of Beaumont, Texas. When the ship arrived at the port, the sailors were given leave for three days.

That Wednesday night, Ovid walked into our church service. He was the first Norwegian I had ever met.

Once again, I experienced the unexplainable work of God. Although I only knew Ovid for a seventy-two-hour period, during that time the Lord baptized me with a godly love for him. Never had I met a young man with such simplicity and purity of heart. He would walk in the ports of the world alone, searching for people to whom he could witness. When his ship would dock in a port, the sailors would all head for the houses of prostitution, that is, all except Ovid. Ovid would walk around, looking for drunkards in the gutters. He would pull them out of the gutters, hold them in his arms, and tell them as best he could, "Jesus Kristus is coming soon."

God used Ovid to inspire me to write the pamphlet on baptism. As dedicated as he was, I still felt compelled by the Lord to explain to him the way of God more perfectly. I felt burdened by the Spirit to explain the importance of being baptized into the name of our Savior. There was one big problem, however—I could not speak Norwegian and he spoke very little English. It was hard to communicate about the most simple things, let alone the things of God.

In the midst of my not knowing what to do, the Lord impressed me to write about the name of Jesus as it relates to baptism. I responded: "Lord, this doesn't make any sense. First, he cannot read English; second, I cannot write Norwegian. Besides, Lord, he is leaving tomorrow, and it would take me many days to write on baptism. By the time I finish, he'll be gone."

In spite of being such a good rebuttal to the Lord's request, my argument brought me no peace. The next day, Ovid set sail just as I had told the Lord he would.

Ovid was gone. But in his place inspiration came—inspiration from the Lord. By then, what I had perceived as a request had become a clear and personal mandate from the Lord. So I set my face like a flint to obey the Lord's instruction, though it made no sense to me.

The Battle with Satan

I was then beginning my second semester of college at Lamar University. It was important that I make high grades as I wanted to qualify for graduate school to earn a doctorate in veterinary medicine. I was still adjusting to college life and needed to study harder in the coming semester as my grades were only a little above average the first semester. Besides, I owed it to my father to make A's since he was paying my tuition.

At the same time I knew Jesus was telling me to devote myself to finishing the pamphlet, and so I did. Day

Appendix: The Road to Ethiopia

and night I prayed, studied the Bible, and wrote. All the time I knew how desperately I needed to be concentrating on my academic studies instead of working on this seemingly meaningless project.

As if that stress were not enough, then began my first real battle with the kingdom of Satan. I did not know what it was to fight a spiritual warfare until that time.

It is said that Martin Luther once threw an ink well at Satan and the stain of that ink on the wall can still be seen to this day. If I had used an ink well during my writing of this work, my wall might well have stains on it, too, for Satan attacked me viciously. My sister, recently related to me in tears that she still remembers how that late in the night—sometimes two o'clock in the morning—she would hear me through the wall, rebuking Satan. So fiercely would he attack that at times it would take two or three hours for me to write just one sentence. But word by word, sentence by sentence I fought Satan, until at last—six months later—I finished the Lord's assignment.

What was my reward at the end? My grades were two F's, a D's, and a drop. All hopes of being accepted into graduate school were gone. There was no way to explain this to my unbelieving father, and my own dreams were crushed.

Just as I finished writing the pamphlet, I was invited to a Christian party in Port Arthur, Texas. There I met my second Norwegian—Gjertrud Kvisvik. She was a secretary and she was fluent in English. When I told her of Ovid Peterson, she voluntarily offered to translate my pamphlet into Norwegian and type it, and she did this at no charge. I mailed it to Ovid's home address in Norway and to his missionary parents in Argentina.

I thought that at last my assignment was over, but the Lord directed me to have it printed in booklet form. Once again, I set out to obey Jesus.

I went to a printer, and he quoted a figure of just over $500. As far as I was concerned, that was the end of the matter, for all I had was $5 to my name and no job.

When I came home, the Lord told me to see one more printer. I did. The printer quoted a cost of $320. He might as well have said $3,200 as $320 was a fortune to me. I could find no peace so I said, "Lord, if you want it printed, provide the money in three days without my having to ask anyone for help."

In two days $220 came from unexpected sources. I was amazed. On the third day, my father walked up to me and said, "Son, I purchased a bond in your name ten years ago. It has matured, and I want to give it to you now." It was for $100—and of all people, from my father!

God's Plan is Fulfilled

In writing the pamphlet, one principle in particular became clear to me—the importance of obedience. I asked the Lord to help me write a poem on obedience to include in the pamphlet and He did.

I gave the printer cash in advance. I expected the pamphlet to be ready in a few days or a week or so. Instead, the printer spent the money on other things. Days passed, weeks passed, months passed—still I had no pamphlet. After about ten months, it was clear that he had no intentions of printing it, and he told me to get out of his shop. But I had obeyed the Lord step by step, and I was not about to let Satan win the final battle. So almost every day after school, I went by until I wore the man

Appendix: The Road to Ethiopia

down. A year later, he finally printed the pamphlet.

I passed out the pamphlets on the streets and mailed others. I thought that was the end of the work. Four years later, however, Brother Urshan read the pamphlet on the Harvestime radio broadcast. God blessed his efforts and many were touched by the message.

In July 1967 Sister Wendell visited our church. Like a little mouse, I slipped up to her, put in her hands a few pamphlets, and then walked away.

Little did I know that I had put into her hands the key that God would use to open the door to Ethiopian revival in 1969. Sister Wendell later related to me that after trying to start a work in Ethiopia she and her husband became discouraged at the lack of a breakthrough in establishing a work for the Lord. They felt led of the Lord to pray and fast. In the midst of this season of prayer, the Lord spoke to them: Remember that boy back in America who gave you the pamphlet on baptism? Take that pamphlet and have it translated into the Ethiopian language.

In faith they obeyed the Lord and the doors opened. In 1971 Sister Wendell wrote to explain, "It was in fact your booklet. . .which really opened the work here." She also stated, "It has been the most powerful help concerning written material other than the Bible. . . .We have wanted to tell you of this so many times, but having lost your name, we could not locate you."

Years later, Brother Teklemariam wrote to me, "I am so glad to tell you that I am very much blessed and guided to the eternal plan of salvation through the booklet you wrote on baptism in the name of Jesus." He went on the explain that Sister Wendell mailed him the pamphlet. When he took it from the envelope, Jesus appeared to him in a vision, leading him to accept the truth written in the pamphlet. His letter to me in 1980 said, "Today there are thirty-five thousand saints baptized in Jesus' name due to that tract."

Brother Teklemariam's wife initially rejected the truth he had accepted. Soon after her rejection, she became seriously ill. While on her sick bed, she began to read the pamphlet. Before she finished reading it, she was healed. She then accepted its biblical message and was baptized in the name of Jesus Christ.

Conclusion

Does God forget our labors and sacrifices for Him? No, a thousand times no! He gives beauty for ashes and the cup of joy for sorrow. For the sacrifice of my grades, He later rewarded me with a doctorate in law with the highest honors the law school confers. Since then, He has blessed me with a wonderful profession as a lawyer, with money, and more importantly, with a wonderful wife, family, and friends. Surely I have experienced the blessing of obedience, and surely I can say, "Thank You, Lord, for battles from my birth to the printing of the pamphlet. All were part of Your glorious plan! Praise be to Your holy name!"

Truly, the road to revival in Ethiopia leads all the way back into eternity, into the very heart and mind of God Himself.